About the Author

Christina E. Foxwell devotes her life to helping others find and follow their passions, transform their lives, and grow into the people they were always meant to be.

Her life's journey began in Port Elizabeth, South Africa and ultimately landed her in Sydney, Australia. Her road to where she is now was paved with hardships and turmoil. She experienced domestic violence, PTSD, and divorce before she found a path to healing and building a life of gratitude, forgiveness, and love.

Currently, she runs a practice called Ignite Purpose, where she has the privilege of guiding others on their life-changing journeys. In addition to her work, she also has many other passions. They include painting, writing, teaching, coaching, and spending time with her family. Her most important roles are wife, mother, daughter, and grandmother of one.

For more information about her and her work, visit her www.ignitepurpose.com.au

CONTENTS

PART 1
The Story of Alchemy & Transformation

PART 2
Weaving a tapestry of love with my story and embracing life's gifts

CONTENTS

I am the author of my story!

*I was never broken; I was
and am on a journey of
alchemy and transformation.
My life is a gift!*

Welcome to
The Glass Angel.

Years ago, I bought glass angels for my Christmas tree. They were so fragile and beautiful. At that moment, I felt like one of those angels myself, but I was imperfect. My wings were broken.

I have a story, which I'll get to in Part 2, but first, in Part 1 I want to show how this glass angel and my story is an analogy for alchemy—the seemingly magical process of transformation and creation. Maybe it's a story that's part of your life, too.

I grew up in South Africa, where I was the daughter of a Pentecostal minister. I had a great love of God, and I knew I had a calling to be a difference-maker.

I did not follow the path of going into ministry at 17 like I thought I might. Growing up, I experienced deep-rooted shame and fear of not being good enough, which set my journey in a different direction. I needed to walk a path that

11

would not only teach me compassion, grace, love and hope but also allow me to give the same gift to others. Maybe this is the greatest calling. To be kind, generous and courageous.

My personal story is about surviving domestic violence, unfaithful behaviour, intense rejection and judgment. It is one of learning how to survive in my world. The greatest gift of my story is about reaching a place where my alchemy was the only choice.

You see, as the Broken Angel, I worked so hard to prove I was good enough. I was dedicated to my career and to making a difference to prove my worth. My intent was good, yet it was tangled up in my pain. I struggled with emotions; I was hard on myself and others, especially if they could not "suck it up". I believed I could push forward and create the world I needed when I focused on my career. I hoped that this commitment would make me worthy and accepted. I found that all the striving, fighting and needing to "be seen" created armour that separated me from what I needed most, which was to accept and love myself first. You can't give what you don't have. Maybe at best you can replicate what you are and put that energy into the world.

My story's painful and shameful parts felt too hard to endure, so I started developing coping behaviours that would numb the pain or make me feel loved. In reality these mechanisms did neither and only deepened the wounds I needed to forgive and release.

What I actually needed to do was realise that I was never bad or unworthy of love: I am me and that is what makes me good enough. Beneath the pain and shame and the armour that protected me—which I called my Ninja Barbie—I was the answer. I needed to accept, connect and retell my story with love, forgiveness, hope and compassion. The story needed to start within me, including forgiveness of self.

As you read *The Glass Angel*, I hope you can give yourself over the metaphor and consider what you might be holding onto that is keeping you wrapped up in your warrior or protected self.

We all can go through alchemy; maybe it's time for your transformation. I wanted to be at peace, and today I am living peace daily and embracing all my gifts. I am grateful. I recognise it's a journey.

Part 1

The Story of Alchemy
& Transformation

The Fall

The rain fell in great big droplets to the ground. The Glass Angel looked up toward the heavens as the cool rain fell on her face. She loved the rain, yet knew with the rain comes storms...

Suddenly, the wind whipped through the air, and the Glass Angel was swept into the dark sky. She desperately tried to navigate her fragile frame as she was tossed like a leaf, to and fro, up and down.

As suddenly as The Glass Angel was lifted, the wind smashed her down, and she hit the ground with a crashing thud. As she opened her eyes, all she could hear was the wind chiming and ringing in a place far away...dull and sharp, clinging and whining.

Excruciating pain poured like hot lava through her body. She looked around in horror and saw broken glass scattered across the dark earth. She knew immediately what she had lost. Curling up against a large oak tree, she started to weep, the sounds of her wailing filling the air. Her wings were smashed, and what remained of them lay glittering in the dark soil. Pain washed over her in waves of agony.

After what felt like hours, the Glass Angel stood slowly on unsteady legs and peered over her shoulder to assess the damage. Her once beautiful glass wings were now only ragged sharp edges, dripping in blood, which splashed onto the ground like more droplets of rain.

She gently picked up the pieces of her wings with shaking hands...the best parts of her, broken off forever. She picked

*She was picking up broken
trust, dreams, courage,
gentleness, kindness,
acceptance, joy and love.
She thought she was picking
up the best parts of her,
broken forever.*

up broken trust, dreams, courage, gentleness, kindness, acceptance, joy and love.

Holding her broken wings tightly, she looked up toward the dark looming sky. "I am broken, ugly and scared", she cried in shame.

She could never again spread her wings and soar through the night sky to catch moonbeams and radiate perfection, joy and light. She could no longer be a real angel.

Looking down at her shattered self, she could see how the other Perfect Angels would laugh at and shame her. These angels remind Broken Angels they should have stayed out of the wind. Their songs of judgement cut deep into the brokenness and never seem to allow healing.

Why do they tease and reject angels who were broken? All angels feared brokenness, yet the compassion needed to accept it was apparently simply too much to ask. So fear turned into shame and judgment, and subsequently meant isolation and loneliness for Broken Angels.

The Glass Angel knew her fate; it was one she had seen many times. It was the one angels feared, and here she stood, broken and bruised, living a nightmare.

The Dusty Path

The Glass Angel looked at her dirty feet in the sand. Where did she belong now? Not with Perfect Angels, who navigated the winds with grace, beauty and joy.

She was now bound to walk the earth, alone and unworthy, and in her mind... worthless.

In that moment, a bright red, silk bag drifted down from the heavens and fell at her feet. She remembered stories of how the Broken Angels were given bags to carry their brokenness.

She sat down and gently wrapped her broken pieces in the red silk. She painfully and slowly wound the silk around her body to keep her pieces close. The sharp edges of her brokenness pressed into her body, piercing her skin and drawing faint beads of blood. The wounds were perpetual reminders of the wind, the fall, the fear, the pain and the shame of being imperfect, unworthy and unloved.

As the sun rose, a yellow glow on the horizon, she slowly stumbled down a dusty road. She had no idea where she was going, yet the path ahead seemed the only way; she could see no other.

She was tired and weary and needed a safe place to rest. As she walked, her tiny feet began to hurt; she could feel their soft thud in the dust, and it was as if hcr feet were the anchors to her flight and were slowly carrying her to her fate. The longer she walked, the more she felt the weight of the red silk bag and her brokenness that pressed and pierced her body in an always-present display of her shame and the pain.

She felt the weight of the red silk bag as it pressed and pierced her body and reminded her of her shame and the pain always present!

After a few days on the dusty road, her legs could no longer carry her. She was exhausted and in agony. For days tears had rolled hot and sticky down her cheeks, and now she felt empty, numb and tired.

At that very moment of realising she could not carry on, she noticed an ancient city peeping over the horizon. Hope flashed through her—the hope of rest. One painstaking step after another, she walked toward that beacon of hope, this hidden city in the middle of the dusty path.

The gate to the city looked as old as time itself. It was awe-inspiring. On the gate, displayed gloriously, were intricate, ancient carvings telling stories of the Broken Angels. These Broken Angels were fearless, hard and strong. They were fighting wars and being celebrated as heroes.

"Oh, this must be the place for me", she whispered to herself. "I might be useful here; I might be able to be worthy again...maybe I have found angels who will accept me. Perhaps I can numb my pain here."

Finding Strength

The Glass Angel raised a hand and knocked on the ancient gate; it resounded like an echo. Hope surged in waves as she waited.

With a whining creek, a tall, strong angel opened the gate. She was glorious.

She carried a blue silk bag around her body, and the hard lines of her face told an ageless story. She introduced herself as Aella, agile and fearless as a whirlwind. Aella welcomed The Glass Angel into the ancient city. All the Broken Angels passed through this city. It was the place where they would be given their names and be taught strength and ferocity. It was where their pain was taken away—or at least expelled outwardly, to reduce the excruciating reminder of brokenness.

The Council of Warrior Angels who ran the city were teachers—teachers on how to numb the pain by staying fierce and fighting one battle after the next to win the ultimate prize. The Broken Angels were taught how to use their pain as a weapon and how to be known for their valour. Through these lessons, they would rise again into glory, just like the Perfect Angels souring in the sky.

The secret hope of every Broken Angel was to be loved and accepted again. To be free to fly in an endless sky. Flying and perfection were only dreams, but learning how to survive was a primal instinct. The council of Warrior Angels were all broken, hard and fearless, and they passed this legacy on to their students.

The arena of pain was where the Glass Angel was taught

to rise. She was taught to numb her pain as she used her broken wings, the shards left from her fall, as weapons. She approached battles with strength and passion, using her small stature to her advantage. She looked so fragile, yet when she rose to battle, she won more times than she fell.

Her red silk bag wrapped around her body continuously drew blood and always reminded her of the reason for fighting. Eventually, she developed the ability to carry the bag with ease. Some days when she was quiet, she could feel the brokenness, and it took her to a dark place. She longed to put the brokenness down, but there was no way. Often she would awake to a new morning with tear-stained cheeks and a heart that felt like it would shatter like her wings.

Every day she spent training, fighting and winning, she developed more armour. She had walked in this ancient city a small angel only wearing a red silk bag. She now wore a bright armoured breastplate, a helmet of gold, daggers forged from the brokenness of her opponents and a large leather girdle wrapped around her to hold her red silk bag in place.

On her final day of training, she was given her warrior name, Shabina, which means "eye of the storm". This name befit her brokenness and also her fierce rising.

In years to come, she became known for her ability to lead the charge and would earn enough gold to live in a mansion on the city's outskirts. She had all she thought she needed to prove to the world she was whole and strong, and yet she was still broken. Still heavy, and still carrying great pain with her.

The numbing she used to win battles lasted only for a certain time, and then when all was quiet again, she could feel the walls shouting her name in jest. She had thought the more challenging the battle, the task or the opportunity, the more worthy she would feel.

She would exchange all the gold in the world to feel whole, free and shameless.

The secret hope of
every broken angel was to
be loved and accepted...
To be good enough

The Call

Her quest seemed fruitless. The more she won, achieved and received, the more she needed. It was like filling a bottomless pit. Always hungry, always needing more. The legacy that followed Shabina was The Fierce One.

The more scars she received in battle, the more Shabina wanted to be perfect. In her dreams, she danced in the moonbeams; she was free, without pain, joyful, and whole! It felt like a cycle from which she would never escape. She longed not to feel the weight of the red silk bag. The armour meant to keep her "safe" was slowly suffocating her light, her feeling. It was as if she was becoming so hard that she was losing the essence of being an angel altogether.

The realisation that she was in a vicious cycle—of needing to feel, and needing to be accepted to be loved, and then using her legacy to "win" the hearts of others only to be caught in the next painful cycle—was terrifying. Something inside was calling her to look at the world differently, yet the shame, fear, anger and disappointment were sticky webs, keeping her locked in. She dreamt of feeling the dust between her toes, the wind in her hair, releasing the silk bag, taking the armour off. She dreamt of being free, at peace, and feeling love, acceptance and kindness.

One night, Shabina awoke from a recurring nightmare where she fell from the sky and landed in excruciating pain and desperate loneliness. Its haunting persistence was suffocating! Rising from her rug in her beautiful curtain-adorned room, she stared out into the desert. The smell of dust and heat even at night was overwhelming.

To clear her mind, she needed to walk. So she adjusted her red silk bag, picked up her armour and slipped out the front door.

As she walked along the dusty road, she was reminded of the day her wings shattered. The day she walked on this very same dry and dusty road. As she walked, she kept telling herself to breathe. Breathe, be free...be light...fly...maybe I can...perhaps there is...HOPE!

A while into her walk, she saw a fire glowing in the night. As she got closer, she noticed someone sitting in the warm glow. It looked like an angel. An angel wearing a golden cloak. As she drew nearer, she felt waves of peace radiating from the angel. Shabina was drawn to the light, drawn to the peace. It was like walking toward a cold glass of water after a hot walk in the sun. Absorbing this peace would quench her thirst.

She thought to herself, "It's like I have been called to this fire...to meet this angel... to feel the peace..."

"Why not sit down", the golden-cloaked angel whispered.

She hesitated for a second, wondering if this was a dream and if it was even safe. Slowly she pulled her dagger from her leather girdle and shifted restlessly.

"You can sit and be at peace; I won't hurt you. I can see you, Shabina, or should I call you Tehila?"

Her eyes widened. "Tehila...no one has called me that since I was an angel in the sky. Tehila means 'Song of Praise', and you can see ME...see Tehila", she softly said.

*The armour meant to
keep her safe was slowly
suffocating her light...*

The Seed of Love

Tehila took a deep breath, recognising the fear that would usually set her warrior in motion, yet choosing to breathe peace. She slowly replaced the dagger in her girdle and asked, "How do you know my name? My origin name?"

The angel looked up and stared into her eyes. She felt such love, such acceptance, such belonging. "I know your name because I have been called to meet with you and share a story."

"Who are you?"

"My name is Ahava; it means love."

"What a beautiful name", Tehila murmured.

"Thank you; love is something we all have, Tehila. I am named after the source that feeds acceptance, belonging, forgiveness, kindness, honesty, hope, togetherness and peace."

As Ahava spoke, Tehila could feel hot tears run down her cheeks. Love was a strange and beautiful concept. After all the years of proving, fighting and winning, and still feeling empty, this simple word filled her with dread and anticipation at the same time. She wondered as she stared into the fire if there could really be acceptance, belonging, forgiveness, kindness, hope and peace for her? She realised at that moment that if love was the source that fed these beautiful elements of life, what had she been living on?

With a shaking voice, Tehila asked, "Ahava, if love feeds beauty in the world, what feeds striving, perfection, judgement, anger, competing, proving and winning at all costs?"

Ahava looked intently at her. "Fear and shame are the roots

*Love is
something we all have.
Love is the source that feeds,
acceptance, belonging,
forgiveness, kindness, honesty,
hope, togetherness
and peace.*

of these behaviours. The fear of not knowing what tomorrow will be, of not having enough, of not being accepted, of being rejected, followed by the shame of not feeling worthy of love and belonging."

"Shame and fear", whispered Tehila. "I have been feeling like I am in a continual cycle of proving I am good enough, of working hard, of needing to be the best, of needing to be seen and accepted...and yet I never felt like I was at peace. My fear of staying out of judgement and shame has kept me running, fighting, winning. It has also kept me alone."

Ahava turned his face toward the glow of the fire. "May I share my story with you, Tehila? It's a story of how I was once called Praelia."

"Praelia!" When she heard his name, she was taken back to when she was training to be a warrior. There was a tale of a fierce, angry, ruthless warrior by that very name. He was the leader of the warrior army and known for fighting with great skill, winning many battles and always ready for the next. He was rewarded for his legacy with fame, money and fortune.

One day he never returned to the ancient city, and no one could find him. There were rumours that he had found grace and peace. That he was no longer the same. The warrior elders quickly squashed these ideas, as they believed the only way to be was just as they had become—strong and hard.

The Gift of Grace

"I am sure you have heard of the Legends of Praelia", Ahava continued as he stared into the firelight. "Actually, the story started with a free, curious and mischievous angel—an angel called Ahava. As a young Angel, I was so playful; I remember being filled with joy and dancing in the sky. I remember looking at the earth in wonder, and of course, my curiosity was endless. So endless that on one night, when the clouds gathered in grey puffs over a roaring sea, I decided to feel what it felt to navigate the wind. As I took flight, I realised I would never navigate this wind. The wind showed me the power of nature in all her glory. I struggled with each breeze; the more fearful I became, the less I could fly. The wind and rain swept me across the ocean and thrashed my body into the ground."

"Tehila, I remember feeling the crush of my wings as they smashed into the earth. I know you know the pain. It scorched me from within. Eventually, I opened my eyes, and as I looked behind me, I realised that where once my beautiful wings were, I now had sharp, rugged, bleeding edges. Their pieces were scattered around me, broken and glistening in the sunlight. My tears fell to the ground without warning. As I cried, I remember promising myself that I would never trust the wind, the rain or anyone but myself. I would rely on only me."

"As you know, we all receive a silk scarf from heaven—mine was purple. I collected my broken pieces and tied the remainder of my broken dreams to me. The pain would remind me never to trust, never to laugh, never to be open to others; it would remind me to be tough and strong."

"On reaching the ancient city, I received my name—Praelia, the ruthless warrior. It suited me because already I had hardened my heart to my true name of Ahava. Fear had taught me to survive through the storm, so fear would be the source of my survival in this cold world. As you know, I became a renowned warrior—one that amounted to fortune, fame and a following. Yet the quiet call of who I really am never left."

"One night, I awoke with the same dream: I was navigating a storm, which thrashed me to the ground. As I awoke, I knew that I needed to be free, free from the self-imposed prison of protection that was slowly turning me into hardened, unforgiving stone from the inside out."

"I remember waking from that dream and walking out into the night, on a road not far from here, I came across an angel named Grace. Grace had a beautiful essence that drew me in—forgiveness and love, for me, so undeserving. Grace allowed me to sit with her. She looked into me and saw Ahava; she reminded me that the angel I had become, Praelia, was only my protection. That the angel I really was would never leave me. The essence of my heart was intact. That curious, kind, beautiful angel was hidden inside me, whether my wings were broken or not."

"As she reminded me of who I really am, I remembered feeling grace and love wash over me. At that moment, my heart started to beat so differently. It beat with peace and forgiveness, with acceptance and love. It radiated hope and joy."

"Tehila, my heart spun golden threads that took each broken part of my wings and put them back in place. Each shard was no longer separate and sharp, but part of a whole, part of what it would always become—a glass tapestry of hope, worthiness, peace and light."

With that, Ahava dropped his golden cloak to the sand,

and from his back rose the most beautiful, imperfectly perfect, golden and glass wings. They were breathtaking in their full, outstretched glory and seemed to pull Tehila closer. It was the gift of GRACE!

No longer broken... Maybe never broken... My life is a tapestry of hope, worthiness, peace and the presence of light!

The Alchemy

"Ahava, I feel so at peace, and yet, I still feel so heavy, so burdened with my pain", Tehila cried.

"Until you allow yourself to be here with me right now, you will never be free", Ahava said. "Until you see your life as a gift, you will always see it for what it isn't rather than what it is and can be."

"How can I see my pain and rejection as a gift?" shouted Tehila. "How can I forgive the angels who laughed at me and judged me for my brokenness? How can I forgive the warrior angels who scared me? How can I forgive the wind, the sky, the earth for putting me in this position? How can I forgive myself! What is the gift in all that?"

Ahava looked into Tehila's eyes and said, "Tehila, when you hold onto the pain and anger, the shame and lack of forgiveness, the cycle of emptiness and searching will never leave: it will swallow you entirely, and you will eventually harden to life, become brittle to the world, and never truly feel again."

"So where do I start, Ahava? I am tired and weary...maybe I should just surrender to the darkness and pain once and for all", Tehila whispered.

"Maybe you can look back at the journey of your life and see the gifts", answered Ahava. "This reflection will allow you the peace you so need, and you will see how your heart transforms and you can be—and always were—whole."

Tehila took a deep breath and stared into the firelight. She slowly reflected on her journey while staying anchored in the present moment. The wind, the earth, the pain, the joy, the hope, the discipline, the ability to live, the forgiveness of her teachers' harshness. The releasing of shame.

As she reflected on shame, she looked at Ahava's wings—so beautiful, so imperfect, so peaceful.

"I am good enough", she whispered. "I am filled with love; I am forgiving; I am kind; I am joy; and my life has a purpose. The stories that were the most challenging have the greatest lessons. There is a gift in everything..." she spoke slowly, letting go of her assumptions and the fear and shame around them. As she did, the red silk bag fell to the ground like an autumn leaf gently swaying in the breeze. Her armour fell to the ground in a heavy thud.

Suddenly Tehila realised that as she embraced peace and love, her heart had started creating the most beautiful golden threads. They came alive, picking up every broken piece and weaving each one back into its place.

When she looked over her shoulder, she saw that her wings were whole and beautiful. They radiated love, joy, hope, kindness, peace, forgiveness and acceptance. They radiated life, and they were so fluid. So unlike her original wings, these wings were even more powerful and held a presence that radiated out of her.

"Ahava, I am me again—I am Tehila!" she cried with joy. "I am free! My fear no longer burdens me; I am no longer broken! Maybe I was never broken...maybe I was on the journey of alchemy all along."

She stretched her wings and soared into the night sky. The moonbeams caught the gold in her wings and radiated light and brightness into the darkness.

"I no longer need to fight for worthiness, acceptance and love. I realise it comes from within me; it was hidden in me all along. I needed to walk my path to learn about grace, shame and freedom. I am so grateful for my journey!"

*I no longer need to
fight for worthiness,
acceptance and love.
I realise it comes from
me; it was hidden in
me all along!*

The Mission

Ahava and Tehila cried tears of joy together. "What will I do with my life now, Ahava?" she wondered.

"Well, Tehila, you now have a choice to do whatever you please. As you know, there is a great need in this world to remind broken warrior angels who they really are. We were not meant to be alone; we were meant to be together, to support each other, to live with joy and to create peace from within. We are called to make this world a better place one angel at a time."

"Where do we live now?" Tehila asked Ahava.

"Well, we live in the world and the homes we have created. We choose to find love, and we choose to see good. We choose to live our alchemy. You see, you will continue to transform the more you do the work, the more you learn about forgiveness and the more you nurture the best of who you already are."

After much thought and peaceful reflection, Tehila whispered, "So I have a mission—I need to help other angels unlock their hearts. I need to help them see that their broken pieces don't mean they are not worthy of love; it means they are perfect in their imperfection. Only when they see who they really are and embrace their story will they be free."

Quietly Ahava stood and handed Tehila a beautiful gold and red cloak. "This will keep your wings safe. It will also remind you of your mission, your calling. It is a cloak of love and hope."

Tehila wrapped the cloak around her. She was ready to

*Only when we see
who we really are and
EMBRACE
our story will we be
FREE!*

share her story; she was ready to walk beside others; she was ready to see the beauty in alchemy.

Tehila joined Ahava and so many other Alchemy Angels in their mission to teach, to share their stories and to help angels unlock all of who they really are.

The Lesson

The story of Tehila and Ahava is one that I have lived personally. The teachers in our lives can allow us to experience healing or challenge us to harden up, be strong and continue the cycle of pain. Yet the gift we all have is one of choice.

The broken shards of the Glass Angel's wings are the stories of fear, shame and separation we have lived and relived without realising. The brokenness represents unmet expectations, broken promises and injustices done to us as well as hurt, pain and rejection.

We will never be free if we keep these stories tied to our worth and belief of who we are. We will keep reliving the fear of what we are not, and we will never be who we want to be. Our warrior self will take over and will sow seeds in our life of further pain, fear and wanting.

I have found that no matter the riches, possessions, success or position we hold, these warrior selves will never give us peace and the ability to love ourselves truly and live our purpose fully.

Are negative emotions and stories destructive? Yes, they can be. If we hold onto these, we will continually search for the next thing to help us feel love and acceptance and to numb the pain so we can survive.

I have also found that the word "love" can be so challenging. I have often wondered why it can create such a visceral reaction in others, in both positive and fearful ways. Then I remember how I reacted to that word. Love felt like a promise of acceptance that I was never allowed.

What is love? I have a few thoughts:

- Love is unconditional, deep affection for yourself and others.

- Love enables us to be open and generous.

- Love lets us be with others.

Love starts inside us, and it's unconditional. I always thought I was giving love while helping others, yet I was providing this help through my own conditional lens of my fear. This meant helping others was a way to not focus on me and what I need to work on, a way to fix what made me uncomfortable. Remove the things that I judged myself on and saw in others.

So, I had become a fixer in my journey. Until I could heal myself, I would always see what others needed to do differently, perfectly or not at all. My shame of what I saw held me in place. I thought if I could "fix" others, then they would be perfect, and I could take their pain away (and I would feel better inside and I would be accepted as good enough).

I know now that we are called to support each other and walk next to each other. To provide options and insights, but to allow others to choose their journey. We are called to sit next to each other in the most challenging times, and to be peaceful and present, just holding the space with love.

We are called to see who others really are. The love we have for ourselves allows us to navigate boundaries and create a world in which we can fully live. A world where we can feel and where we can feel with others (empathy, connecting emotionally and feeling what others are feeling).

Love starts
inside you and me and
its unconditional.

Reframing our life as a gift... will help us release shame and embrace ourselves

My journey on this path has taught me many things:

- We were not meant to be alone; we were meant to be together.

- Our strength to protect is less effective than the courage we need to show up and show who we are every day.

- Our imperfections make us beautiful, and the acceptance of our own and others' imperfections allow us to create a tapestry of what it means to be human.

- Boundaries are critical, and using our voice to share what is okay and what is not okay allows us the opportunity to encourage openness and honesty.

- Recognising the stories that bind us to our pain and the triggers that can pull that pain back into focus is part of our healing journey.

- Reframing our life as a gift is the greatest gift we have, and it will help us release shame and embrace ourselves for who we are and life for what it is.

Part 2

Weaving a tapestry of love with my story and embracing life's gifts

Embracing My Story

We all have a story, and I didn't realise the extent of my pain cycle until I was sitting at the airport in Melbourne a few years ago and was worried about my husband and our marriage. You see we were in a cycle of not speaking, living past each other, and getting caught in our own negative stories. I was worried I would relive heart break, rejection and being alone. Let's not mention the shame of what others would say if our marriage failed!

I have the kindest, most caring husband. Yet I had not learned how to put my warrior armour down when discomfort arose in our marriage.

You see, John is my third husband (Technically my fourth, as I married my first husband twice). I felt like marriage was an area in my life that I would never be good at. I was always scared, always in protection mode and always waiting to be hurt and disappointed.

That moment in the airport, I felt hope run through my hands like sand. I was so afraid, drained and hopeless. As tears ruined my makeup, I remember seeing this image of myself in my mind: I was "tarred and feathered" because of my shame and the judgement I had received from others—and that I had given myself. I thought my life was shameful and I was shameful. I repeatedly told myself the lie that I wasn't worthy of love.

Until this moment, it was as if my shame was following me like a paintbrush, painting a shame trail! I couldn't escape

*"The change I needed
had to start in me"*

it, and it was ruining my joy and happiness. I could no longer outrun or outwork my shame. It was time to walk into my story, accept it for what it is, forgive myself and the others involved and find the gift to free me and subsequently heal us.

The Beginning

Over the last few years, I have spent time working on my thinking and looking for the threads of my story that were created when I lost the essence of ME. The time I started to forget who I really am. Why don't I start my story with where I was born?

In 1974, I was born in Port Elizabeth, South Africa. I want to share with you the beauty of my parents. My dad, Charles, was so passionate about his calling, and his intense love for God has been sewn into the fabric of my life. He was also my daddy. I looked up to him; I loved him. He was strict and had great expectations for us as we extended his ministry. My daddy has passed on now; I miss his hugs, prayers and love for me.

My mom, Dawn, is pure JOY! She is fun, cheeky (I know where I get it from), hardworking, caring and creative, and I have always known she loves me. She would protect me with her life. I hope that soon she can live with me full-time and I can care for her. My mom and dad loved each other, too. I had a home filled with love where we feared God and worked in the church and community.

As I reflect on my story, I forgot that my parents were human, not superhuman, and they were imperfect just like everyone else. They strived to live their purpose and a godly life. They didn't have all the answers, and today I am grateful they did their best and my life has become a gift in part thanks to them!

I was looking for the threads of my story that were created when I lost the essence of ME. (my shame roots)

Losing The Essence of ME

Until recently I always knew there were different sides of me. One of love and compassion and one of protection and anger. What I have found is that the *essence* of me isn't fearful and protecting. The essence of me is beautiful, just like the essence of each person I meet.

Later in this book, I will share the activity (practice) I have done to find my essence. I used a picture to remind myself of who I really am.

The picture is of myself and my brother sitting in a rockpool while on holiday when we were around four and five years old. I am looking at him with such joy and love. I am happy, joyful and carefree, and I know I am loved. There is nothing in the world I can't do. The essence of me is all of these beautiful things.

What I now know is that I had forgotten that beauty within me, the inner person who knew she was loved and good enough. I forgot who she was because I had to learn how to survive in my world; even with all the good around me, I had to walk a stony path (a shameful path), and just after this picture was taken, my life would take the course that has now led me to my healing and continued alchemy.

At the age of five, I was molested by a family member. I can remember it happening, and that it felt surreal. I told my parents right away, and I think it was tricky for them. They loved me so much, yet didn't quite know what to do. I thought they didn't believe me and that maybe I was just dreaming. The situation was uncomfortable and scary.

I remember my parents listening yet they only put me back to bed. I remember speaking to my mother about this years later. She asked me if it ever happened again, I said no. Yet as a young child I felt I was bad and unsure of my reality.

Being a parent myself, I know the battle of being challenged when shameful things happen and you struggle to understand what to do, so you do what you can.

I did what so many of us do when something bad happens to us, I had buried this story; I didn't want to think about it. It made me feel dirty. In order to be free, I needed to own it.

About a year ago I spoke to my beautiful mommy, and she acknowledged the memory. She and I have talked about the memory with much love. I am sure after reflection that my dad addressed the family member, as my dad was always filled with courage.

Thank you, Mommy, for the willingness to speak about it and the love that we can share as we recognise it for what it is and accept it to be free.

What we didn't realise back then is that a child who goes through something like I did needs love, care and acceptance. Instead, when things like this abuse happen, we respond with and experience SHAME!

As parents, we experience shame, and the child who has been violated experiences shame.

Shame is a horrible feeling, and none of us likes it. When something awful happens, we shy away from shame and separate ourselves from others. The stories of not belonging and not being good enough start playing through our minds, like "The Never-ending Story." That darkness swallows up light.

We grow shame in secrecy, silence and judgement (Thank you, Dr B Brown, author of The gifts of imperfection). The shame root constricts our mind, thinking and behaviours. My shame was becoming the darkness that would slowly direct my journey as I developed coping behaviours to feel better.

To be free, I needed to start by digging up my shame root.

My shame was becoming the darkness that would slowly direct my journey as I developed coping behaviours to feel better.

The Key In Me!

As I was doing that internal reflection work and fully realised the situation, I got angry. Maybe MAD is a better way to describe it.

I felt an injustice had been done to me. Once I thought of this family member, I couldn't stop. I didn't want to let it go. About 18 months ago, as John and I walked and talked and reflected, I told him it was time for me to forgive them and let it go. My anger and lack of forgiveness were making me bitter, and it was dulling the essence of who I really am. It was keeping me locked away in fear, shame and protection.

I had to accept that violation happened; I had to choose to forgive the person and recognise that I am not that story—it happened to me, and I can choose how I think about it. Only I can dig out the shame root and start untangling my heart from its grasp.

It may be easier to hold on to bitterness and an unforgiving stance, yet both of these feelings harm us and fortify the separation we create from ourselves and those we love in our lives.

Upon reflection, I am grateful for my story; I am grateful because I can connect deeply with others that have experienced this pain. I can also rejoice, as having this experience has allowed me today to live my purpose fully with love and compassion.

*It's easier to hold on to
bitterness and unforgiveness,
yet both of these harms us
and fortify the separation
we create from ourselves and
those we love in our lives*

Shame Roots Grow

This was the start of my walk in and through shame (The feeling that there was something about me not worthy of love and belonging) and the feeling of being aware of sexuality (from the abuse and being awakened) without realising it.

Sexuality and being awakened at a early age will create behaviours that will cause the deepening of shame and judgement both in self as well as with those around us.

Before speaking to my mother about being molested, I felt it was a dirty little secret, my shame.

After much reflection, I realised the darkness had given birth to this time of my life. If I didn't address, connect with, and walk through that darkness, it was a root that would keep growing and create loops, cycles and nooses in my life.

Here is the worst part of my memory about the abuse: I can't forget it. I remember it like it was yesterday, and before healing it was a feeling of being dirty sticking to me like a second skin.

If I didn't address, connect with, and walk through that darkness, it was a root that would keep growing

A year after it happened, I played "Doctor, Doctor" with the neighbour's twin boys, and we were found out (we were examining each other's bodies!). My dad was so ashamed of me. I remember receiving a few hard blows from his shoe, and I felt dirty, shameful and bad. I think that was the first time I experienced being truly terrified. I wanted to run and hide and never be found. I was so embarrassed (though maybe shame is the better word to use here).

My negative thinking and internal judge learned to shout. I had created shame for my family. I was bad; I was not good enough. They say shame is like being burned with hot water. I agree; the scaring from shame is excruciating.

Wearing Masks

To survive in my world, I developed the coping behaviours of people-pleasing (never saying no, needing to be liked or gaining approval) and being restless (always busy) —they ruled my life. I had friends in high school that said I should just be myself! What did they mean? I didn't have a clue who I was...

To be accepted and live in my world, I needed to be the minister's daughter, a good girl. My community growing up—where my dad was the minister—was primarily Dutch Reformed, we were not. At school, we were seen as a sect (or even a cult). It was so stressful growing up with the gradual realisation that you are different from others because of what you believed. We could not join the Christian group at school, as we were not seen as the same. I remember being friends with the Jewish kids and how I loved being with them. I felt accepted. One thing I could do well was sing. I participated in the school choir, eisteddfods and school productions. It felt like this was one place where I could use my gifts to be loved and accepted. Yet I had fallen into a worthiness trap of people-pleasing.

This people-pleasing continued in my life as I grew older and started taking over—nothing felt like it was ever enough to fill the gaping hole of belonging. So, I needed to wear masks to serve others, turn the other cheek and be the better person. Never set boundaries, never use my voice in a way that would displease.

Because I struggled with boundaries, I didn't know what my voice "was". I lived in a blended world where using my voice was not something I was allowed or something I even dared to do. Actually, I become an expert at hiding. I knew how to be invisible, especially at school or in social settings outside of church and community.

The only place I felt safe and where I do believe I shone was in our world of church, including both the ministry and being part of the community. This place of safety was also a place of fear for me; because of my heightened sexuality I always felt like a sinner. My coping behaviours didn't help either, and the need to be loved and accepted would eventually create chaos in my world.

These masks were meant to keep me safe, to hold the "dark" hidden and to show the world I am good enough. The problem is is that a mask separates you from both others and living in general. I am so grateful that I know these fears for what they are now and I am free to take the mask off and be me!

Under the mask was the opportunity to own my fear of the dark, to remember who I really am and to have the courage to be seen, heard and valued. I still have to stay present because the mask can so easily slip back on. Only through my mindfulness practices, am I healing and transforming.

So where is the gift in all this reflection? Recognising that separation is a human condition, but an avoidable one. We can teach others to not wear masks because to see and be seen is a vulnerable experience. The only way to truly live is to put the mask down.

The only way to do that is to start by looking inside first. To recognise we are not our stories, we are not our thoughts and fears, that everyone has a story.

Maybe the opportunity is to start being the answer, maskless and naked.

*Under the mask was the
opportunity to own my fear
of the dark, to remember
who I really am and to
have the courage to be seen,
heard and valued.*

Starved of Connection

I remember years ago saying to a boyfriend that I wish I knew how to be a friend. I didn't know how to be in a friendship connection. It always made me feel unsafe and a little on edge. This alone must get you to realise that I would have "masked up" in friendships just in case they saw me. Or hurt me.

As a little girl, I remember being carefree and making friends with many people. The older I got, the less I was able to engage in connection. Why? My battles of self-worth and belonging had taken over. I had learned how to starve myself from connection. I was suffering from acute loneliness and didn't know how not to feel so alone.

How often are we with a group of people, family or friends, but we are suffering and feeling so lonely on the inside?

Last year I discovered the work of Vivek H. Murthy. He has written a book called *Together*: *loneliness, health and what happens when we find connection.*

For the first time, I got it! I have suffered intense, or even worse, acute, loneliness. It started when my shame root showed up and overtook my ability to be with others, let them get close and share simple friendships. I was terrified of being hurt, judged or rejected—or having them find out my shameful secret.

The strangest thing was, though, that I was okay with connections in my work world, where there were boundaries around my activities, tasks and relationships. I also had a Ninja Barbie armour that protected me.

*Accept those threads in
my story that feel bitter,
shameful and painful
and turn them into sweet
forgiveness and freedom.*

But what that armour did was slowly separate me from others and starve my essence, which needs connection to thrive. I was hard on myself, pushed myself to "achieve" and I was hard on others. Which only made my loneliness worse.

According to research, there are three "dimensions" of loneliness:

Intimate / emotional loneliness:

- Longing for a close confidant or partner with whom you can share a deep, meaningful bond.

Relational / social loneliness:

- Longing for friends, companions and support.

Collective loneliness:

- Longing for a community to share your purpose and interests.

Boom: it hit me. In order to feel less lonely in any of these dimensions, I had some work to do on shifting my "connection" habits. And the only way to make space for that shift would be to acknowledge and accept those threads in my story that feel bitter, shameful and painful and turn them into sweet forgiveness and freedom.

That process would take courage. The courage to put my mask down, the courage to be me.

Bittersweet Threads of Connection

I could share so many stories I have had to walk through to turn the bitter into the sweet, but in this chapter, I will tell a few that particularly impacted my ability to connect and kept me locked in isolation. I hope these stories can inspire you to turn your bitter threads into sweet ones and give you hope that you can turn your loneliness into connection.

The Gift of Self-compassion

Living in a Pastor's home is never easy; as the family, we are constantly watched and expected to lead by example. I am grateful I grew up with such responsibility, yet it had its challenges.

One of my bitter threads that unravelled was in high school. A new boy joined our class. I was friendly and sweet, and we started chatting.

Later that day, a few friends told me I needed to be careful as he was into satanism, and they told me a few stories of what they had heard. I had never met anyone like him before, and actually, I quite liked him—he was sweet too.

That evening at dinner, I started speaking about the new boy and what my friends had told me. My dad was immediately worried. I know he loved me so much and wanted to protect me and do the "right thing."

The next morning my father called the principal and shared his concerns. The school took immediate action, raided this boy's locker and found all his satanic practice items. They expelled him. That very day during a school assembly, the headmaster thanked me personally from the stage for my actions that got this boy expelled.

All the school kids, my friends, my brother's friends, strangers—everyone—wanted to know how I could do that. How I could tell on him and get him in trouble. I remember that suddenly I had no friends. I had no one that would speak to me. I was lost in a sea of unfriendly faces. I felt like my life was over.

The pain and the shame of the situation severed connection and left me alone. As I relived this memory in my healing journey, I recognised it as one of the strands that, if accepted, I could rebuild trust in myself and with others and subsequently rebuild connection with courage and trust.

What do I now accept?

- This memory is in the past, and the trauma and fear I experienced are also. I am safe.

- I forgive myself for sharing the story at the dinner table. I think I felt I had done something bad, so I had such guilt and shame.

- I also forgive my daddy for wanting to protect me and stand by our beliefs.

- I send love, compassion and courage to my 15-year-old self.

- I recognise that I am wiser now and that I am good enough—to be loved, to be connected with—and that I can allow others to see me, love me and care for me.

Acceptance and Self-love
allow us to honour ourselves
and embrace our story with
forgiveness and compassion.
Only then do we become free!

The Gift of Love!

My second bitter thread involves my divorce.

I grew up in a community where I led the youth group, directed worship and ministered with my musical gifts. I think back now, and I realise that this community was the only place where I felt safe and had a purpose and role. I married my high school boyfriend at the age of 21.

Our marriage had challenges and joys, yet I walked away from our marriage when our daughter just turned two. At that point, we had been married for nearly three years. I moved back home and lived with my parents, yet my parents openly discussed that I could no longer be part of the ministry and use my talents. I was getting divorced, and I had left my husband due to a short-lived relationship with someone else who had shown me kindness.

I realised, based on our beliefs, that my parents were right.

It was hard not to feel shame. Shame that I had cheated, shame that I could not use my gifts anymore since I had sinned, and shame that my sin would forever be a scar on my life.

A few months later, I transferred my job to another city, a 12-hour drive away from my parents, my ex-husband and my community. I was hoping to leave the shame behind and hoping that I could join another church where I could find my acceptance and belonging and use my gifts. I had a real shock when the people I met would give me a wide berth; I was a single mom with a little girl at the age of 25.

One person told me that I needed to stay on my knees and pray that my husband would change and that I needed to repair the marriage. That would be the only way to be accepted and to be back in my community. I was shattered. My shame was following me—it was the blemish on my life, and I would not find acceptance and love in my community any longer.

I was often phoned by family members who gave me biblical scriptures that I needed to repent and change my life or be cursed. I was lost; I didn't know what to do. The black fog of pain was choking me; I felt there was nowhere for me to be safe, to be seen, to be loved, or to belong.

I was a single parent living far away from my family and desperately looking to rebuild my life. Yet my loneliness was becoming excruciating, and I needed to self-protect. The community I had always felt so connected to didn't know how to love me; they only knew how to judge and shame to support their discomfort of my life.

A while back, I sat in a church service and wept; the tears kept coming. I know that God loves me, yet the judgement of people and my community had told me that I was not good enough for that love or their love anymore. I realised that I needed to start healing from this story or it would rob me of being peaceful, being connected to God and being part of a community—or even being brave enough to allow others to be close to me.

What did I need to accept now?

- To forgive myself for cheating, as I now know it was going against my values. It's not the "me" I wanted to be. I now recognise this action as a restless coping behaviour.

- To forgive my community. Their beliefs were keeping them locked in fear and judgement over my "sin".

- To forgive my family for not knowing how to love me and support me as they were wrestling with their own shame and fear.

- This was my past, but I am free, and the messages I was telling myself about not being good enough to be accepted are lies. I am good enough, I am good in general, I don't have a scar of shame across my chest, and I am beautiful in my imperfection.

The gift of this thread is that I now know I can show love and grace to others that have gone through similar pain. I listen without judgement, and I can set boundaries that hold others' judgements away from my heart.

My community and my love for God is not only in a church—it's in people who love, care and connect. I am building my new community and am so grateful I have the courage to step out of loneliness and into love and connection.

It takes courage to put down Shame and to set yourself free! You are worthy of love and connection. You are good enough and deserving of all the beautiful things in life.

The Gift of Freedom

Free from the Shame of Domestic Violence.

Boundaries and knowing who we are are key to living a wholehearted and healthy life. Living to please, avoid and overcompensate can create patterns of unhealthy relationships with yourself and others.

My first husband was from our community. His parents were in our congregation. I remember being great friends with his brother, who is the same age as me. My future husband was the golden child of his family— excellent at rugby, and everyone loved him. He was also reticent. That's what I remember most about him when we were kids.

Fast forward a few years, and even though we moved towns, our families reconnected. I was sixteen, and he was eighteen. I remember he liked me, but I was unsure I wanted to date him. He had teased me relentlessly during a family visit, and I remember not being comfortable. So, I chose not to date him.

Instead, I dated another boy whom I adored from our youth group. Thinking back now, that relationship was where I started trading my worthiness. He broke up with me at youth camp, leaving me heartbroken and swimming in shame. I wish I could whisper to myself back then that I am and always was good enough and that I need to remember who I am. I now acknowledge the gift I can give myself based on this story. I can recognize the patterns of fear that caused me to create coping behaviours. To release those behaviours, I needed to walk through the story and love me more than anyone else could.

Coming back to the story of my first husband, I remember picking up the phone and calling him, an action fueled by a broken heart and a needing to be loved. I asked him on a date, and he was there in a blink. I remember him arriving at my home in his police uniform; he looked so brave. Almost like a hero!

Instead of healing myself, I was looking for someone to make the pain go away. And so began my journey of codependence.

Let me define Codependency:
A codependent person feels a deep lack of worth. In order to feel worthy, they will do and say what they need to in order to be loved and accepted:

- They willingly give their voice, choice and sense of worth over to another in order to be accepted.

- They submit to servitude and obedience to be accepted

- They need to be needed

- They loose their identity

- Their identity is the relationship

- They reduce their wants and needs and struggle to express what they want or need

The enabler is the partner to the Codependent:

- They feel satisfied that their needs are met

- They start expecting the sacrifices and neediness

- They become bigger than the codependent and in doing so set into an unequal partnership

- They need to control more and take charge more

- Their needs become more important and therefore they keep enabling the cycle

In my codependence, I was slowly losing my identity. I wanted to please my first husband and to be loved by him. His teasing became personal, and I was never able to be good enough. My parents were unable to send me to university, and I was unwilling to explore further study even though I could do it. I lost more of my self-confidence.

My parents started noticing a change in me and shared their concerns. I didn't pay any attention to them—all I wanted was to be loved by and cared for by this man. He was a rising rugby star, and he was a hero (riot squad policeman).

I now know that my shame and fear from my past (the root of my sexuality and worthiness) was showing up and feeding the codependence I was building.

We got engaged when I was 19, and I remember him proposing on the beach. I was so excited the ring popped out of the box onto the sand. He immediately got really angry with me for how stupid I was to drop it like that.

I remember feeling such bittersweet joy. You see, I realised at that moment that this marriage was possibly going to be hard for me. I was even more determined to show him I could be good enough, perfect even!

The gaslighting started here, and the systematic breaking down of my confidence was in full swing.

Gaslighting is a form of manipulation that often occurs in abusive relationships.

It is a form of emotional abuse where the person gaslighting makes the person they are engaging with question their sanity, their judgement and their worth.

If the gaslighter is questioned they can punish the other person by silent treatment, sarcasm, outbursts of rage until they are once again in control.

What's the impact of being gaslighted?

- You start to feel unsure of your perspective of your world
- You wonder if you might be imagining things or being oversensitive
- You could even question how sound your mind is (your sanity)

Gaslighting can be displayed in the following ways:

- Lying to you
- Discrediting you
- Distracting you
- Minimizing your thoughts and feelings
- Shifting blame
- Denying wrongdoing
- Using compassionate words as weapons
- Rewriting history

Of course, our brain is wired to survive, and I was going to survive at all costs. During our engagement, he was called away to do border patrol for a few months. For the first time in a few years, I felt free! It was so strange. He did telephone me frequently, and our arguments seemed to grow.

In reflection, I think he felt I was moving away from him, and I was starting to feel I could be more. (I was breaking the codependent cycle)

During this time, I was working as a receptionist at a distribution center. We had a new manager who decided to take a keen interest in me. I was vulnerable; I was so uncertain of myself and continuing to fight an inner battle of being good enough.

I was asked to work late one night and was told this manager would drop me off at home. I was 20 and naive. I agreed and was so flattered. While locking up the office he cornered me between a security gate and the office door. Suddenly I was in a situation I didn't know how to handle.

I didn't set boundaries and didn't say no (I didn't know how not to please!). He was twenty years older. I was young and caught in a horrible situation. You can well imagine what transpired.

In reflection I was being taken advantage of by being made to feel special. Until the #ME TOO movement I have thought maybe I was the bad one!

I was stuck, I was in a situation that was not aligned with my values, and I was wobbling. What actually happened was I was a victim of abuse and assault yet in my mind I translated this very differently.

In my mind I had failed! I immediately broke off the engagement. I felt lost, ashamed and needy. I needed the codependence—I just could not live without it. I thought it helped me stay true to my values.

Within six months, my first husband and I were back together, and shortly thereafter we got engaged again. This time, I told myself, I would follow through. Yet this time, I was also told to lose weight—that I was overweight and fat, and in order to make him happy, I needed to be thin. I had to pay a price for my shaming him.

When we got married, I weighed 45kg. I was the smallest I have been. My wedding dress was almost too big for me. I would do anything to make him love me, forgive me and take away my shame of being incongruous with my values.

On reflection now, I can see how misplaced my solution was. I needed to heal, to look inside, but I had a habit of running away from my shame. This habit would become a consistent coping behaviour in my life—trying to outrun, outwork and escape shame.

Little did I know I was running into a very dark place. I am still grateful, however, for this time in my life. I conceived my daughter on my honeymoon, and she is one of my greatest blessings. I now also have a grandson named Charles, and he fills me with joy.

I don't think you know you are suffering from domestic violence until it's too late. If you are in a codependent relationship, you almost need the control, or else you can't function. It's a vicious cycle of bad behaviours fueling one another. My abuse wasn't visible; I didn't get hit by his fists, I didn't have bruises on my face, but I was controlled. What I did, whom I spoke to, and what I could and could not eat were dictated by him.

As we drove away on our honeymoon, I was told how things were going to be.

I was not allowed to contact my parents without his explicit permission, and he was now the head of our home. I remember listening to the rules and being overwhelmed.

He would control me through silent treatment or through tirades where I would hear how worthless I am. I felt like an empty shell. The more control I gave over, the less "me" I was. I thought that relinquishing would please him. Instead, this seemed to make things worse.

I started getting really scared of letting him down. While pregnant with my daughter, he would go out partying with the rugby lads after a game, and I would be at home, pregnant and alone. I started realising that he was being unfaithful when I developed an infection. It was so horrific—he told me I was disgusting and falling apart. I was mortified and so ashamed of what was happening to me.

I had one person that was allowed to be close to me, and she was my sister-in-law, who still works with me today.

I gave my salary over every month from my 9-5 job as a personal assistant. I cooked food at night. I tried to keep the house in order. I made sure I wasn't giving him any trouble.

I would do anything to avoid being in trouble or making him unhappy.

I had moments of absolute frustration, where something in me wanted to fight to survive. I remember getting so angry I actually packed my bags. He would simply wait for me to stop fussing. I would never leave—he owned the car, how would I leave? Where would I go, that would mean I had to tell others my story. This thought and the fear of judgement kept me in the marriage.

All I wanted was to be loved, and I traded my worthiness on a daily basis to keep the peace and to be acknowledged. Anything for a kind word.

At around eight months into our marriage (I was also very pregnant at this stage), I found out for certain that he had been unfaithful.

In some ways, I felt it was what I deserved, because of our breakup while engaged. Yet I also still felt broken and less than good enough. I had met the young woman at a family gathering. She had joined his sister, who was visiting from out of town. She was attractive, with long legs and long hair. I felt round, pregnant and unattractive. I didn't realise what happened until I was told by my sister-in-law. She felt it was unfair and that I did not deserve his behaviour. I was heartbroken. I was so ashamed.

When I confronted him, the gaslighting was in full swing. His favourite saying was: "believe what you want to believe." I thought I was losing my mind. I wanted to be a mother, I wanted a loving partner, and I wanted the white picket fence story. I was slowly losing myself.

Now I could say you should feel sorry for me, but that is not the purpose of my sharing my story. I am sharing because at the time, I didn't realise how I had given myself over to control and verbal abuse. I didn't realise the thought patterns and trauma reactions I started developing during this time. Ones designed to keep me alive!

During my maternity leave, I was locked into our apartment, and he would check on me at lunchtime to see how I was. I would love to have spent time with my mom at this stage to get her to help me. He forbade it. My mother could visit me once a week. I felt like I was slowly losing my will to live.

I remember walking into his closet hugging his clothes and sobbing. Wishing he would never come home again and then hating myself for thinking that. I just had no courage or money or know-how to leave him.

When my daughter was around a year old, he told me I needed to choose between him and my parents. Upon reflection, my love for my parents and their protection of me was not easy for him when I needed to submit fully.

It was the most challenging time of my life. My parents were not allowed to be with me. I was unable to greet them or spend time with them. So, I started sneaking visits with them. I don't think it's a choice that should ever be made. I was slowly being isolated and cut off.

He fed me many harmful messages during this time, but these are some of the most consistent:

- You are fat and only I can love you.

- You are a bad mother and wife.

- Only I can take care of you.

- You are coloured—check her gums, everyone. (Having grown up in South Africa, his comment was meant to shame me and was racist)

When my daughter, Carolees, was one, I got hired by an investment company as a receptionist. I was so excited and hoped I could do well. This company paid monthly bonus payments; I didn't realise what that meant until I received my first paycheck.

I received more than double my pre-tax salary into my bank account. I was so excited and so conflicted. I had always paid my salary over to my husband and he would give me pocket money every week, so I was totally reliant on him. Suddenly I had money that I didn't need to tell him about (or did I?).

During this time, I fell into my niche. I was good at investments and customer service. I loved the challenging conversations. I loved finding money in trades. I started taking work home on weekends and sorting out customer investments queries. Within six months, I was the Customer Service Manager for our branch. I went on my first business trip to Cape Town. I was FREE! Even it if was for short amounts of time. I, of course, would pay for that freedom with silent treatment and insults when I got home, but it was worth it—because for the first time in a long time, I could breathe.

I slowly started realising I was more than the horrible things that had been said to me over the years. That I could be someone...maybe I already *was* someone. The more I developed in my work, the more control he lost.

Around this time, one of our friends decided to make a HUGE confession to get the guilt off their chest. They called me at the office and told me they had had sexual relations with my husband, and also with his entire sports team at the same time. They cried and asked me to forgive them.

I was shocked and angry. I called him and told him not to come home. That this time I was done. He once again used his ability to convince me that he would never do that, and that this person had just tried to hurt me.

I knew it was the truth, that this person was telling me a fact—that "truth" had often been written on the teams' faces when they looked at me in pity. I was the cute little trophy wife who was incredibly obedient and dominated.

This confession made me work harder at my job, and yet another coping behaviour was born—my ability to achieve results and throw myself into my work instead of facing a personal challenge. In work, things are ordered; I could set boundaries, have difficult discussions and play by a set of rules that felt safe. I was also paid for my effort, and money meant independence. Coping or not, I was so unhappy.

Codependency eventually robs you of your identity. You become a shell of a person. You lose your voice and your essence. You become a slave. Perhaps most significantly, you lose any sense of having a relationship with yourself.

I must shine a light on the story here. I did have moments during this time where I would shout and cry. Where I would fight for my rights. But these moments were intense and unpleasant. I was stuck in a cycle of pleasing, obeying the rules, failing the rules, being punished and pleasing all over again.

I realised things were starting to unravel and my life might actually be in danger when we had a rather challenging argument about my being English and his wanting me to speak Afrikaans. When we were kids, his family were in our Afrikaans assembly. We grew up fully bilingual, but my schooling was in English. So, when I spoke to Carolees in English as a baby, he got really angry with me. He wanted me to raise her solely speaking Afrikaans.

One night our discussion escalated and before I know it, he was strangling me against the wall with my little baby crying and holding onto my leg. Why didn't I leave...where was I going to go? I couldn't imagine telling anyone what was going on. Would they even understand? The worst moments were when I wondered if it had even happened. Maybe I was lying to myself. All the gaslighting was making me question my sanity.

During this time my nanny (our domestic worker named Lilly) was my friend and would do anything to protect me. I remember leaving the car radio in the car instead of taking it out with me after attending an Easter service rehearsal with Carolees (who was a tiny baby).

The car got broken into and the radio and rugby gear were stolen. Lilly stood between me and my husband to protect

Only I could set myself free
I need to own my part
in my life with love
Choose to recognise my worth
Be brave to love me first!

me. He was so angry, and I was so grateful for her love and support. She saw me and she loved me.

At this stage of my story, I want to press pause.

You see, you could get angry right now based on how I was treated. I want you to remember this is my story and that I am owning both the good and the bad. He has his story too.

I cannot tell you what he needs to own and accept; I can only tell you the change needs to start in me. During the time we spent together, and post that, I developed PTSD from trauma. This seemed to keep snowballing until I finally started to heal and own it. I needed to own my shame story. I needed to own and release my pain. I needed to forgive. Until I did these things, I would always be owned by the story versus recognising I am not the story.

Moving back into the story, it was time for my coping behaviours to reappear. Instead of learning how to put the bags (shame stories) down and be free, I seemed to keep adding weight to those bags and running deeper into shame.

Our marriage ended when I met someone else and had a short (one night) interlude with them. I know that this was a crazy time, I also recognise that had this not happened, I don't think I would have had the courage to leave. This person reminded me of who I really was. They gave me compassion and kindness and for the first time in years; I felt like someone actually saw me. We did not end up together, and yet I was very honest that I had met someone else. My parents said I could come home, and that's what I did.

Rinse and Repeat

A really great heading for a codependent: you can't live alone! I tried; I found the following:

- I didn't know how to work with money.
- I was lonely.
- I needed to be controlled to feel safe.
- I didn't know what food I liked.
- I didn't know what I liked to do.
- I didn't know how to be without someone else being my all.

This part of my story I call the "rinse and repeat" era. Why? Because that is exactly what I did!

After a failed post-divorce relationship in a strange town, I got robbed by this man. I then moved into my granny's one-bedroom apartment, and with my little girl, we lived on her enclosed balcony.

I am so grateful for a wonderful grandmother like her. Evelyn Christina Cilliers, you were remarkable. I thank God for you. You took me in, you tried to cook for us even though you could barely see (often we ate burnt food!). We lived on the smell of an oil rag (living on very little money).

For three months we stayed together. During this time, I think she could see I was giving up. I know she didn't know what to do to help me. The reality was that she could not help me; *I* needed to help me. I remember being so depressed that my life seemed pointless; the burden of my shame was too heavy.

At this time my ex-husband's mother passed away unexpectedly. We started talking more, and Carolees missed her dad terribly. One day he called and said that he believed he had changed. That he knew he had done wrong by me and that he made his mother a promise. I was so tired and so hopeless that I listened to him. I wanted to trust him. I wanted not to worry about money or people's judgement. I had that voice from my church community ringing through me. You should have stayed on your knees and prayed he will change.

And so, rinse and repeat started. He picked us up and took us back to our hometown. He was so happy to have his daughter back in his arms. I was happy to move back to a life I was hoping would be different. I still had the scars that told me otherwise, but when you are exhausted, and you feel worthless (as you were told you were) you give in. So, I did. Anything to have a bit of normality back in my life.

My parents reminded us we needed to be committed to living together, so we did "the right thing" and got married for the second time. I remember walking down the aisle and feeling such fear. That very day the crazy started again. There was family drama at the wedding. Shame and all the unresolved emotions bubbled to the surface.

As we settled into our life together, instead of working through our challenges, we decided to party, drink and live it up. I now know this behaviour was a form of numbing pain and fear. What a crazy time. Thinking back now I realise and own I was numbing. I think he probably was, too.

The last five months of our second round of being married were horrific. I was always in trouble. There was always drinking, and I was seeing him at his worst. We had lost respect for each other.

It was like a phoenix rising from the ashes of my story, my pain was my fuel, as I look back I am grateful for this time in my life...

Our codependence was short-lived, as I started to push back. The final crushing straw came during a BBQ with his rugby team—he lost his temper with me and dragged me down the passage by my hair. Our house emptied as people quickly left. No one came to my defense. No one helped me.

At this stage I was no longer in love with the white picket fence. I was in reality land where the conflict, shame and paying back of pain was intense. I could paint a wild picture of things that happened, but I finally decided to give in to the pain and take my own life. I knew I didn't want to be with him. I knew I couldn't go through the shame of leaving him (what would people say). I thought the best way was to leave him with his daughter and remove myself from the picture.

I tried to take my life by drinking mild pain pills. It didn't work. I left him a letter and he was so angry with me. He told me how selfish I was and how pathetic that I couldn't even kill myself.

I felt ashamed and helpless.

At this stage, I was working at Coca-Cola as a personal assistant and business analyst. I met and fell for one of the Regional Sales Managers. (A subconscious escape plan.)

I hope you are seeing my cycles repeat. I can see it repeat...instead of rising once and for all into my healing and finding help, I kept looking for someone to love me. I was a codependent trauma victim who was vulnerable and not really ready for a relationship. And yet that is exactly what I pursued. I was looking for someone who could control my world, give me stability, but also allow me to be free.

I adored this man, and yet I know he wasn't ready to be a father to my daughter and a healthy partner to me. We were ill-suited, and when he left us after two years together, it was traumatic...but it was also time to rise. You see my Ninja Barbie was about to be born and take over, as my pleaser had simply not "cut the mustard".

I moved out of our brand-new double story home into a friend's spare room. We had no other place to go. For the third time in five years, my daughter and I were in a cycle of hopelessness. The difference this time was that I was about to rise, and this rising was, without doubt, my saving—and also the heaviest armour to wear.

I was tired of getting hurt; I was tired of needing a man to save me. I was ready to save myself and my daughter. I think of my rising and I am grateful, even though it cost me joy, love and connection. I focused on achievement, I focused on building a wall around me. I was so unhappy, and I used my ability to numb my emotions as a weapon to fuel my drive. I was starving myself of the need for love, for connection and joy was a luxury I wasn't allowing myself. Pain was the fuel to take me out of my situation.

Birth of the Ninja Barbie

The birth of my Ninja Barbie (my fully armoured self) was a gift at a time when I really needed it. My trauma was an open wound that wasn't healing, and my survival brain was activated to find a new way to survive.

I decided that I needed to live by working hard and not trusting others, especially men. I was hard on men. I wanted them to pay for my pain and to feel the shame that I had been given in spades over the last few years. So, I decided to play with their feelings, not get too close, work hard and take care of my daughter.

I was isolated in a new way. I was isolating with coping behaviours, and actually, I was isolating from kindness and love. Upon reflection, I can see why and how I did it.

I needed help and my parents referred me to a counsellor who lived in my city and who was a minister too. I decided to see him.

I remember he reflected on how I was carrying around painful and shameful stories in my heart. Stories that I had not made peace with, that I needed to let go. Oh boy, trigger moment!

I wanted to hold onto these painful stories. They were the fuel I was using to power myself forward. I didn't care if they were hurting me; the more I held onto them the stronger I become. Or thought I became. I wanted to use them as reminders of my shame and therefore as justification for my behaviour and thinking.

Me and my son, my gift, Joshua.

My fuel was my pain
My reality was survival
No deep Joy, No peace
I needed to release it all,
I call this the gift, Grace!

Can you see how when I hold only my negative stories, they can cause rising/ surviving and also great sadness? (It's the best way I can describe the emotion).

The more we use these stories as our fuel the more we stay in survival and the less we learn how to thrive.

Yet there is no real good or bad, there is learning, and I call this Grace.

Small Moments of Grace

Isn't it wonderful to recognise that with pain there are always moments of grace?

See, I could look at this time in my life as being only filled with pain, yet there were moments that gifted me HOPE!

Maybe the kindest thing others can do is love you when you are down. Stand next to you and pick you up. Not fuel your shame but give you the courage to show up for your life, even if it's for the small moments.

The work-family that kept me from total emotional collapse was the beautiful Kelly Pretoria team. I must say that my focus on helping others allowed me to love my role as a Temp Consultant. At one stage I had 100 temps working for me across offices in Pretoria. These employees were mainly women, and they gave me much purpose. They also inspired me—to rise, to fight, to live. They showed me they could navigate life even with very little, so I could do the same. They never shamed me, and they become my friends.

I believe that purpose allows us to see past our own pain. Through this time, I became a rescuer rather than a supporter. I could focus on helping others so that I didn't need to help myself (which would mean owning how I was feeling).

Only later in my life would I see that these rescuer tendencies can be the traits of my Ninja Barbie.

"Maybe the kindest thing others can do is love you when you are down. Stand next to you and pick you up. Not fuel your shame but give you the courage to show up for your life"

Friends who stood next to me in my journey, who supported and loved me. *Top left*: Wendy Phillips, my leader and hope giver. *Top right*: Anel Jacobs, my sister, kind, caring and a lioness. *Above*: Yolande Kruger, my friend, fearless and compassionate.

The Rescuer vs the Supporter

If you have unresolved trauma like I did, you can show up as a rescuer—otherwise known as a "fixer". Our trauma can also be passed on through our parents—their behaviours, their coping mechanisms and their DNA.

So as my Ninja Barbie took over, I did the following in order to feel I was good enough:

- I took responsibility for things that didn't belong to me.

- I made excuses for others' behaviours.

- I took the blame for others' actions.

- I provided unsolicited solutions and advice.

- I put my needs aside (which I had learnt to do as a codependent pleaser).

Why?

- I struggled with my "good enough" measure from a young age.

- I was codependent as my way to serve and be loved.

- I didn't know how to sit with my own trauma and shame, so I tried to outrun it and dull it by trying to "fix" others.
- I was feeling guilt and shame for my decisions, behaviours and actions as I navigated my survival.

What has my journey of taking power away from my Ninja Barbie allowed me? It has allowed me to heal, to walk through my story with courage. To become a supporter, not a fixer. I must tell you it's a journey, and as soon as I realise, I am fixing, I can re-align and remember who I am.

Being a supporter looks like:

- Actively listening and empathising. Staying in the moment with others and being curious and open.

- Acknowledging what we can't control. The only thing we can control is who we are, how we think, what we do and how we show up. So, I need to work on myself first.

- I need to be okay with the idea that others need to learn from their mistakes, and that process belongs to them. My role is not to fix them or make them better; my role is to bring the best of me that I can and help them step into growth for themselves.

- I have to honour others' decisions when they don't want my help or support. That is not a reflection on me; they will choose their own journey.

- I need to own the greatest gift— working on myself.

Bottom line: the change always starts in us first!

"*I need to be okay with the idea that others need to learn from their mistakes, and that process belongs to them. My role is not to fix them or make them better, my role is to stand next to them!*"

The Impact of Ninja Barbie

When my judge, the Ninja Barbie, shows up, I am stuck in fear and judgement. How did this armour manifest in my life?

I lost feeling. I struggled to love. I especially struggled to give love to myself. I wanted to show the world what a powerful, strong and independent woman can achieve.

One of the first things I wanted to do was have a baby. I wanted another child, and I didn't want to be married. I always felt that I would have a little boy, so I set out to find a man who would help me realise my vision.

I met my son's father a year and a half after I moved into an apartment with my daughter. Of course, I have many stories of this time in my life, which I will undoubtedly share in the future. I was attracted to his wit and his mind. What I didn't realise was that our pain and trauma had pulled us into a relationship of convenience more than love.

I fell pregnant really quickly and we decided that we would give this relationship a go. We would treat it like a business partnership, and we would choose to love and live together.

We were living a social experiment of our own making. A hastily blended family with my eight-year-old daughter and his six-year-old son.

At this stage, my career also started taking off, and my Ninja Barbie started protecting me in new ways.

We decided not to get married, but we would live together. I purchased a house in my own name, and I hoped I could trust this man and trust that our emotional experiment would see us into a happy future of our making.

While pregnant with my son, I fell ill with gallstones and had major surgery. There was a possibility that my son would not survive, and we had 3D scans to meet him. Joshua looked just like my dad! I felt such joy and love for this little boy I had chosen to have.

The relationship between my son's father and I become quite volatile. He lost his job during this time, his ex-wife was suing him for higher maintenance payments, and I was carrying most of the expenses. I had to "rise" to keep us alive, and I had the story that you could never trust a man replaying in my mind.

When Joshua was born, I drove and checked myself into the hospital. I was paying for his birth independently. I was proud of my independence and recognised that I would have to be independent to survive this next chapter of my life. I found that I could be cold, clear and direct. I trusted only in me.

I have to admit I treated my son's father with little grace during this time. His circumstances and his relationship with his ex-wife and their codependency made me uncomfortable, angry and sad.

My parents moved into our home shortly after my son's birth. They were a gift in an uncertain time. They helped me by taking care of the house and kids while I worked long hours in my career to earn money and independence.

Do you know money can't fill the gap and make you happy? Money and even a fulfilling career, without healing and growth, just lead to a continued worthiness battle.

My parents wanted me to live a Godly life and deep down I wanted to do the "right thing", after much consideration we got engaged and I married Joshua's dad. We stayed married for a year. During this time, my career sky-rocketed, and I was independent. The marriage/relationship we set up wasn't working for me, and I don't believe it was for him either. In actual fact, I was very unhappy and unfilled.

I was spending a life with someone that I didn't love and respect. I know much of this situation was part of my story, and some of this was part of the story we created together. My Ninja Barbie was running my life. I was armoured up, strong and pushing myself. I felt I needed to be the provider and that my family needed to trust in my ability to bring home enough money for us to live and thrive. You see, by this stage I had lost trust in his ability to be a partner contributor in our home and as I reflect, he was doing the best he could, yet I was feeling unsafe.

I made many mistakes during this time. One was developing the coping behaviour of shopping! I know a few of you must know that feeling? This behaviour was killing me financially and drawing me into an anxious place. I was not taking responsibility for my life and owning my pain and finding my healing. Instead, I was working, spending and fearing. I didn't know how to make things better.

It needed to start in me. Not feeling (recognising my emotions and understanding me) was slowly blocking my ability to feel deeply, and I started to yearn to be seen.

My relationship with my son's father was broken down. He was drinking a lot; I was working a lot. We spent very little time together. I was leading a team and loving it. I was smashing goals in the workplace, and I was able to connect with my team. My parents were helping me raise my children and run my home. My beautiful friends were keeping me together. (Thank you, Anel, Wendy and Yolande.)

I didn't want to end the relationship; I tried to ignore our problems. I didn't want to recognise that I needed more than simply sharing expenses and responsibilities.

Even if my Ninja Barbie was protective armour I needed

"Even if my Ninja Barbie
was protective armour
I needed to shed "her" in
order to heal and grow,
my armour would slowly
suffocate all the good I have
to give the world and leave
me empty and hopeless"

to shed "her" in order to heal and grow, she taught me some valuable lessons:

- Be true to yourself and own your emotions.
- You are mutually accountable for the good and the bad.
- Forgive yourself for not using your voice or being more honest and clear.
- Celebrate your son as your beautiful gift.
- Recognise that what you felt made you strong was slowly suffocating who you really are.
- Communication, boundaries, honesty and love are the keys to living.
- Growth has to start in yourself first. By setting yourself free, you set those around you free, too.

New Beginnings

I want to celebrate new beginnings with you. I met my husband, John, at the end of my marriage to my son's father.

For the first time in years, someone saw me, and I allowed someone close. John knew I was married and was very clear he would not get involved with a married woman. His values are one of the things that have made me better and helped me heal and love.

I decided to embrace the fear I had been nurturing for a long time; I chose to navigate a new path for my children and me. For the first time in my life, I felt I could make a few bold moves. I realise today that some of these moves were my coping behaviours, some were courage, and some were Ninja Barbie moments. I am grateful for doing the best I could.

After building a friendship through email and video calls, I decided to visit Australia, where John lived. We spent two weeks talking, laughing, crying, exploring and connecting over our stories.

On my return, I applied for roles in Australia, and in two months, I had a firm offer with a visa. Later that year, I moved to Australia with my beautiful children to charter a life in a new country, with the hope of deeper love and an opportunity for my children to live their dreams in a country that had so much to offer.

*Embracing my emotions,
getting curious about my
story and working on me
is what I can control—
and it's worth it.*

I have so many stories of my journey in my new home country, but here are some of the most powerful discoveries:

- The dream and the reality are not easy to navigate, but with growth, healing and love, it's possible.

- Unless you work on your healing and growth, your patterns will keep repeating and further embed shame and fear.

- Embracing my emotions, getting curious about my story and working on me is what I can control—and it's worth it.

- Being brave and stepping into life to live it with passion and courage is what we are called to do.

- Putting our shame down allows us to heal and be free.

- Lighthouse moments (those uncomfortable, challenging moments that help us see clearly through the fog) are here to teach us. Don't get triggered and stuck—learn, connect and be the answer.

- Judging others' stories is not what we are called to do. We are called to listen, learn and be with others.

- When we judge, we have something to learn about ourselves.

- Find that safe place to share your story, to own it and then to free yourself from it.

Embracing my emotions, getting curious about my story and working on me is what I can control—and it's worth it."

My Life, the Gift

I believe my story in Australia is a book in itself. I will share this in my next book, *Living Bravely in the Arena*.

This book has been designed as a three-part journey. Part One, the story of the Glass Angel; Part Two, my story of alchemy; and Part Three, a few practical tools to help you reflect on your alchemy and growth and to learn how you can be FREE!

Years ago, I was reading something Dr B Brown had written—that you could be the author of your story. That you can own it and rewrite your story. I remember saying yes, yes, YES!

For years I have been a relentless researcher of myself and of others' working on healing and growth to understand how to unlock my self-imposed prison of shame and fear and how to live free, to be me, to be all I am, to use my gifts, to love deeply and to teach others how to do the same.

My greatest wish is that you have been able to embrace my story with love and grace. What has happened is in the past. A client who heard I had been married a few times said, "I didn't know you were that kind of person." At that moment, I realised that her thoughts had tumbled out of her mouth. I asked with grace, what kind of person was that? She realised

Only I can…. unlock
my self-imposed prison of
shame and fear and how
to live free, to be me,
to be all I am

that she had judged me. It was my lesson to learn that I need to recognise that in sharing my story through my lens, your judgment triggers might have gone off, yet I also realise I am good enough for love. I am healing, and it's my story without shame

You see, we all want to be accepted and loved. My greatest learning is that acceptance and love come from me first—and yours must start from within, too! I am the key to my own story, and so are you to yours.

I look forward to sharing tools and insights into growth in Part Three.

Part 3

Alchemy Practices

Doing the Work

Welcome to the final part of this book. Practices of Alchemy are important to help you transform your life. As I have shared in my story, we can either stay stuck in the cycles of belief, thinking, emotions and behaviours—the ones that impact our ability to connect with others—or we can choose to break the cycle. Only we can break it because our perspectives, stories, experiences and what drives us starts in us.

I would always say the first step is to recognise your motivation as a key to any transformation. My motivation came from a place of pure exhaustion and realising I was in a cycle of protection that no longer served me and that kept me locked away. I felt tired, prickly and overwhelmed by negative emotions. These emotions spilled out into all aspects of my life. I was like a mouse on a wheel trying to outrun and out-prove my own fears.

This weekend I was driving in the car with my husband and reflecting on how peaceful I was feeling. In that moment, I recognised how much pain I had been living in for so long. Prior to my journey of alchemy, fear and internal self-conflict were constant companions.

I don't think I was very present in moments with myself. I couldn't sit with myself, my thoughts or my emotions. I needed to dig deep and let things go. It's a journey.

A participant in one of my mental fitness programs asked me if I was able to stay in a peaceful space the majority of the time now that I had done the work.

Oh, what a great question, one that I took up with my coach (yes, a coach needs a coach). I reflected on the ebb and flow of our lives and how much I would love to be in a peaceful space 100% of the time. Then I remembered...I am a HUMAN!

I had started beating myself up with the simple question of if I was really walking the talk; I needed to be ZEN—almost inhuman and perfect. I am smiling as I write this line, because I think that the ebb and flow of life is the polarity of living. (Like breathing!) Why did I feel that I needed to be the perfect embodiment of my work versus the learner of my work as I continue the practice? I wanted to quiet my own judge. Only I can, and not by proving but by accepting I am doing the best I can every day.

So, before we get into these exercises, let's remind ourselves that we need to learn the practices that will allow us to dig deep, uncover those skeletons that we forgot, pull out our shame roots and be in the light where love, joy and peace live. We can't expect to be at peace 24/7, but these exercises will help you bring more of it into your daily life.

These alchemy practices are based on cognitive behavioural therapy (CBT), acceptance and commitment therapy (ACT) and performance coaching reflections. They will help you do the work on yourself because you *matter*, and when you do, you can unlock your purpose, be better with others and become a learner of transformation and positive impact. You can be free: dance in the rain, feel the wind in your hair and wrap your arms around yourself first!

Your next steps:

- Grab a pen and marker and create some "me" time. You want a calm environment to start your reflections on how these alchemy practices can unlock you.

- Be open to understanding yourself—without judgement! —as you learn about yourself, your behaviours and your life. Learning is a place where you don't judge yourself as a failure or unworthy of connection. It's a place where you take perspective, get interested and become willing to own how you showed up, the story you told yourself, the beliefs you hold and the emotions you feel. It's a place where you choose to be brave and start embracing the ME you already are—the ME that is hidden behind your fear and armour.

- As you go through this journey, why not touch in with your coach, therapist or someone who loves you unconditionally and has done the work on and in themselves? Someone who will hold space for you. Choose wisely and always start with yourself first. You have to love yourself passionately and recognise that you matter. Always.

"we can either stay stuck in the cycles of belief, thinking, emotions and behaviours— the ones that impact our ability to connect with others—or we can choose to break the cycle."

My Values and My Beliefs

Having come from trauma, I realised that in order to heal, I needed to understand my beliefs and how these were impacting my thinking, my emotions and my ability to connect with others. I also needed to understand and reframe my values, which had translated into deep pits of self-judgement and judgement of others. I needed to understand those values and connect them to love versus using them as my measuring stick of "safety", protection, acceptance and being good enough.

Definitions always help us with understanding meaning.

- *Beliefs:* Based on our experiences and thoughts, beliefs are assumptions we hold as our truth— they do not have to be fact-based.

- *Values:* Based on our beliefs, our values help us take action based on what we believe is essential to us. In other words, they are our motivation.

It can be very difficult to understand what our beliefs are, so we might need to start by defining our values. Once we know clearly what our values are, we can dig deep into the "why" of them and start to understand our beliefs and thoughts that have contributed to these values—and subsequently see if we can shift the original belief story. You see, we sometimes think WE ARE our beliefs and our story. We are not our story, and we can rewrite our beliefs and change our life.

The first time I did a values activity, I was at a Brene-Brown session in Sydney. When I was asked to list my values, I chose things that were really important to me, like hard work, commitment etc. What I didn't realise was that I had a few deep-seated fear and protection beliefs that were feeding these values, and those underlying beliefs were keeping me locked in a world of running and proving.

In order to be good enough, accepted, seen and not judged I needed to value:

- Working Hard

- Being performance focused

- Serving others

- Being seen as tough and strong

In turn, I believed in order to be good enough, accepted, seen and not judged—and to fulfill these values—I needed to:

- Celebrate work-a-holic tendencies and be driven by achievements at my job.

- Avoid being well-rested, because that meant I wasn't working, which meant I wasn't earning. Earning meant safety.

- Give to others beyond what I had in my tank, because these sacrifices would be considered good deeds and would drive acceptance and love.

- Achieve my goals to gain promotion, and through that I would be able to take care of my family and anything else life could throw at us.

If you look closely, there's one thing all these underlying beliefs and top-level values have in common: they're driven by fear.

*We are not our story, and
we can rewrite our beliefs
and change our life*

I am not saying that all beliefs are negative and are fear driven. We are wired to survive as humans; our brain keeps us in a state of survival, and sometimes in being driven by survival, fear takes the wheel, and we miss our opportunities to thrive and live a purposeful and fulfilled life. Since I have done the work in me, I have shifted some of those ingrained biological fear messages.

I love working hard, yet I recognise that that does not make me successful. My life is rich when I spend time with those I love. My son needs a hug over an extra $50 in his bank account. I need connections with friends and family, not building all my time around work and focusing on gaining a return and forgetting that I matter.

So how have my values changed? Let me share two examples of how I worked to reframe my values and the beliefs that underline them.

My foundational value is LOVE.

I believe that by loving myself and taking care of myself, I am able to be there for others. Love allows me to connect without fear rather than exchanging my worthiness and to recognise I can be all I need to be when I think and act from a place of love.

Another value I hold close is DISCIPLINE.

I believe that showing up is how I walk my talk. Showing up allows me to achieve goals both in work and in life. I engage disciple because I choose to be brave even when I want to hide. Why? Because I am worth it.

There are lots of positive, fulfilling values that you may choose as your foundation. I have added a list of values that you can reflect on. That might be important in your life.

Values

Acceptance
Accomplishment
Accountability
Accuracy
Achievement
Adaptability
Altruism
Ambition
Amusement
Assertiveness
Attentive
Awareness
Balance
Beauty
Boldness
Bravery
Brilliance
Calm
Candor
Capable
Careful
Certainty
Challenge
Charity
Cleanliness
Clear
Clever
Comfort
Commitment
Common Sense
Community
Compassion

Competence
Concentration
Confidence
Connection
Consciousness
Consistency
Contentment
Contribution
Control
Conviction
Cooperation
Courage
Courtesy
Creation
Creativity
Credibility
Curiosity
Decisive
Decisiveness
Dedication
Dependability
Determination
Development
Devotion
Dignity
Discipline
Discovery
Drive
Effectiveness
Efficiency
Empathy
Empower

Endure
Energy
Enjoyment
Enthusiasm
Equality
Ethical
Excellence
Experience
Expressive
Fairness
Family
Famous
Fearless
Feelings
Ferocious
Fidelity
Focus
Foresight
Fortitude
Freedom
Friendship
Friendship
Fun
Generosity
Genius
Giving
Goodness
Grace
Gratitude
Greatness
Growth
Happiness

Hard work	Patience	Solitude
Harmony	Peace	Spirit
Health	Performance	Spirituality
Honesty	Persistence	Spontaneous
Honour	Playfulness	Stability
Hope	Poise	Status
Humility	Potential	Stewardship
Imagination	Power	Strength
Improvement	Present	Structure
Independence	Productivity	Success
Individuality	Professionalism	Support
Innovation	Prosperity	Sustainability
Inquisitive	Purpose	Talent
Insightful	Quality	Teamwork
Inspiring	Realistic	Temperance
Integrity	Reason	Thankful
Intelligence	Recognition	Thorough
Intensity	Recreation	Thoughtful
Intuitive	Reflective	Timeliness
Irreverent	Respect	Tolerance
Joy	Responsibility	Toughness
Justice	Restraint	Traditional
Kindness	Results-oriented	Transparency
Knowledge	Reverence	Trust
Lawful	Rigour	Trustworthy
Leadership	Risk	Truth
Learning	Satisfaction	Understanding
Liberty	Security	Uniqueness
Logic	Self-reliance	Unity
Love	Selfless	Valor
Loyalty	Sensitivity	Victory
Mastery	Serenity	Vigour
Maturity	Service	Vision
Moderation	Sharing	Vitality
Motivation	Significance	Wealth
Openness	Silence	Welcoming
Optimism	Simplicity	Winning
Order	Sincerity	Wisdom
Organisation	Skill	Wonder
Originality	Skilfulness	
Passion	Smart	

Practice 1

Reflecting on Your Values and Potential Underlying Beliefs

Consider the list of values and highlight ten words that you think reflect what drives and motivates you.

....

....

....

....

....

....

....

....

Reflect on the ten words you have selected. Which of these are truly and deeply connected to what drives you every day? See if you can reduce the ten to five core values.

Take a moment to consider and write down what values do/ did your parents or important authority figures have? How were these values displayed in their life? How might they have shaped your own value selection?

Next list out the underlying beliefs you have that link to the top five values you selected. Do any of these stand out as being linked back to the values your parents displayed or past trauma and experiences in your own life?

....

....

....

....

....

....

....

What fears, stories and judgements do these values and their underlying beliefs and assumptions place on you and others?

....

....

....

....

....

....

....

Thinking beyond your own experiences of these values, what does living these values look like when coming from LOVE, when they support your and others' mutual success?

"We are wired to survive as humans; our brain keeps us in a state of survival, and sometimes in being driven by survival, fear takes the wheel, and we miss our opportunities to thrive and live a purposeful and fulfilled life."

Digging into Your Beliefs— Catching Moths and Butterflies

Our thoughts stem from our beliefs, which form our values, which continue to drive our fear stories and judgments.

So, to recognise our beliefs and why we have them, we need to understand what we are thinking—and why.

We can shift our beliefs—and therefore our values and our stories—only if we know how that belief was formed and choose to accept, reflect and redefine it.

Imagine being the author of your story rather than having to be a character in one that was written for you by your past experiences?

When I realised, I could be the author of my story, I was so excited. Some of the stories I have told myself based on a belief have taken me into a continued cycle of drama that subsequently reinforced my beliefs. It can be a vicious, self-perpetuating cycle. I needed to activate the circuit breaker, and it started with my acknowledging the stories I tell myself and how those are based on my beliefs.

I call this process catching moths and butterflies. "Moths" are negative thoughts that form negative beliefs that lead to fear-driven and protection-driven values. By contrast, "butterflies" are positive, reflective thoughts that form positive beliefs that lead to values driven by love and acceptance.

Our "moths" tell us we need to survive and protect ourselves. When we are in this headspace, we cannot be open, curious or willing to explore and see. We end up judging and hurting ourselves, which also means we judge and hurt others. There is always an impact and an outcome. These "moths" simply reinforce my fear and protection beliefs and values.

I found I could have short term success in this cycle, but there would be a toll on me and my mental fitness and agility in the long term. There would also be a toll on my relationships, because I would isolate myself from others and end up lonely in a crowded room when I am in survival mode.

Let's start on the next Alchemy practice ...
Based on your beliefs, you have stories. These stories are your thoughts. They keep you safe, but they can also keep you locked into fear.

We all have a story wrapped up in fear thoughts, those things we tell ourselves when we need to protect ourselves or stay safe. If I listen to these thoughts, I stay "small", and I will lack the courage and confidence to show up and live my life. Instead, it should be about embracing and experiencing both celebrations and challenges and recognising that these moments don't define me; they teach me.

If you find yourself stuck within your fear thoughts, maybe it's time to rewrite your "moths" as "butterflies" in acceptance and love.

Here are a few examples of mine to show you how you might make this shift in belief.

The Lie 1 (Moth):

You are not white and you won't be accepted—hide, protect, and prove you are good enough.

I looked just like my dad with olive skin, chocolate brown eyes, and dark hair as a child. My brothers were fair-skinned and had blue-grey eyes. I grew up in South Africa during Apartheid. The colour of your skin mattered in simple ways that affected daily life, like being able to get restroom keys at gas stations, sitting with your parents at a rest stop, and people wondering if you and your dad were not white if you were with your Mom and brothers. You wish you were white like others around you. You feel like you don't belong—like you are less valued.

In my adult life, I was often taunted by my first husband at parties where he asked people to "check her gums" because "she isn't white" as if that were an insult. Now that I am much older, I realise these remarks weren't something to hold onto as shame, but that is how I felt, and I struggled to love myself because of it.

The Truth 1 (Butterfly)

You are beautiful, carmel, and you are perfect the way you are. Your colour does not define your worth or your value. You look just like your precious dad and granny. You can love yourself for who you are; your love for you will help you love others, too.

You have experienced separation in your life based on your skin colour; you can be a difference-maker now and speak to inclusion and connection beyond race and colour and even religion.

The Lie 2 (Moth):

You have been divorced a few times; there must be something wrong with you.

In my life, I felt my divorces were my scarlet letter painted on my life. My shame was a brush that I seemed to drag behind me, colouring everything I did. My thoughts aimed at both men and anyone who judged me were always of embarrassment, justification and hate. I told myself I would never be free to love and be loved. I would be like Elizabeth Taylor with many ex-husbands, and I would keep losing because maybe I never deserved love anyway.

The Truth 2 (Butterfly)

Your past is not shameful. You have made decisions based on what you believed was right and part of your survival. You were in a cycle of pain and relied on past strategies to navigate people and not allow yourself the most incredible love story, the story of loving you first. It's time. It's time to forgive, accept and free yourself from the scarlet letter and that shame brush. Your divorces do not define you, and you are not them. You are transforming, and through your transformation, you are rebuilding courage, bravery and freedom to be who you are. You can now walk next to others going through challenging times and connect deeply with empathy and compassion.

The Lie 3 (Moth):

You are not a good mother—you work too hard.

Having navigated my life as a single and struggling parent, I realised the only way to take care of my family was to be financially independent. I had a little mantra I would repeat to push me along. No work, no pay, no food TODAY. While raising my daughter and navigating financial hardship, I would count every cent. I would keep money in envelopes with labels to ensure I had enough to take care of my responsibilities. This fear of not having enough food or essential money drove me to work long hours and be hungry to prove my worth. It was also a belief that would turn into a value of hard work. My survival instinct was to work long hours to create career progression and financial return. That fear of "not enough" seeped into my way of life.

The Truth 3 (Butterfly)

You have worked long hours through troubled times to take care of your family and build a life. You have sat on aeroplanes in the early mornings crying because you miss your children. You are a kind and generous mother. You have done what you needed to when survival was on the cards. You have always held your babies tight and whispered in their ears you love them. You have always provided for your family. You care for your children, and by caring for them as much as you do, you are now on the road of alchemy, to heal your wounds, to realise that working non-stop has caused health issues and that your children need a mother, not a memory of one. You recognise when you are in fear and forgive those who judged you because of your dedication. You are a wonderful mother, wife and daughter; celebrate loving them, Tina!

The Lie 4 (Moth):

You are fat, and no one will love you, so keep being unhealthy; it's your body.

How ugly are your legs and your round body? You are not good enough and to help yourself sooth you need to eat the

135

pain away. When you eat you feel better, and that Chocolate and Cake make you feel good. You just need to listen to the cry of your hunger and feed yourself. Being unattractive and overweight will also keep you safe. You won't be prayed on by men who want to use you. You can stay out of your own way by staying slightly overweight. Anyway, you work so hard you deserve to over-eat and spoil yourself. It's too hard to try and you will fail!

The Truth 4 (Butterfly)

When you were a little girl, you had this beautiful soft little body. You have struggled with pain and discomfort, and through that, you have learnt to numb by eating. You have created habits of self-soothing that have been detrimental to your health. It's time to love and nurture. your body so that you can be healthy, happy and peaceful. It's not about failure it's about self-reflection and self-connection every day. It's about making better choices because your health is important. As you evolve with deep self-love and care, recognise that you are worth breaking the cycle. You can be healthier by becoming peaceful and catching the habit in action. You are worth a long and generous life. Embrace your worth.

These were my stories/ thoughts and beliefs...I could fill a million-page journal with them. It's a daily reflection practice of being peaceful, calming my mind and recognising the thoughts that don't serve me.

Negative thoughts and emotions are meant to keep us safe and alive. If we believe them and hold onto them as the truth, we can get stuck in endless cycles of pain and coping behaviours.

When you start recognising your inner critic and the fearful voice in your thoughts—we all have an inner critic or judge that encourages us to beat ourselves up and build our Warrior Angel—you can begin to rewrite your story one truth at a time.

In the following few pages, you will work through how to see who you really are and how to reflect on acceptance beliefs that will help free you and remind you of who you are with love and compassion. Remember, you are not your thoughts or your story. Keep journaling, reflecting and being curious without fear.

Practice 2

Catching the Moths and Creating the Butterflies

What are 3 statements you repeat about yourself that hurt, harm and keep you small? Write down these statements and try to trace back why you may have them so ingrained.

For each of these statements, reflect on how you have done your best and how you can relook at your story from a perspective of compassion and gratitude. Consider what you have learned because of these experiences. Write a short paragraph that celebrates your journey of learning, self-discovery and truth.

Three statements you repeat to yourself:

1. Reflection:

....

....

....

....

....

2. Reflection:

....

....

....

....

....

....

3. Reflection:

....

....

....

....

....

....

....

....

Self-Love

What a wonderful and challenging concept. Yet it is the key to looking at your life with compassion and love. You might need to keep relooking at your moths and butterfly stories as you continue to transform and heal. As you continue unlocking the ME you want to be, the ME that is already in you.

During my first walk through the Positive Intelligence program, I was asked to do a self-love and exploration activity and when I did tears ran down my cheeks. Why? Well, I had forgotten the beauty of ME. The ME before I realised, I needed to protect and fear and before I was doused in shame. Below is my picture; I am three, and my brother Paul is four.

When I look at this picture of me, I see joy, light, laughter, love, cheekiness and freedom. I see ME. This is the beautiful, imperfect ME—the essence still inside me. Our fear thoughts, experiences and beliefs create a cage or armour that locks the core of who we really are inside. I had forgotten the essence of who I am.

As you catch your moths and create butterflies, embrace that essence of you. I am now embracing ME and allowing ME to BE to SHINE and to SHOW UP! Meet TINA!

"When you start recognising your inner critic and the fearful voice in your thoughts—we all have an inner critic or judge that encourages us to beat ourselves up and build our Warrior Angel—you can begin to rewrite your story one truth at a time."

Practice 3
Embracing YOU

Find a picture of yourself as a young child. This picture will be your anchor to help you remember the essence of yourself. Looking at this picture, write down the words that come to mind. Who was this child before you needed to protect, fear and hide in yourself? Spend a bit of time doing this activity and return to it throughout your alchemy journey as needed. The more you connect with your younger self, the more you will remember and fall in love with who you really are.

Below paste a picture of yourself as a young child, one that you can see all the beauty of you...

Write down what you see as the essence of you, the beautiful parts that you know are inside that shine through at times, yet these parts are hidden by your armour, fear and shame. Consider these essence elements of YOU, consider how it will be if you could bring them to life every day? How you will live, love, lead and thrive?

What others will experience with you? What will you experience in yourself?

I have experienced, peace, generosity and deep love for me, which has helped me have deep love for those in my world. This has helped me reduce the power of my judge (or as I have called her my Ninja Barbie!).

The essence in ME is: ... (Write down the words that come to mind when you look at your picture.)

What would your world look like if you brought more of the essence of YOU Into every day work and life? How would you feel?

Recognising Your Emotions and Their Impact

When we struggle to recognise our emotions, we don't understand how we are feeling, why we are feeling this way and what to do with our feelings. We also don't learn that our emotions are connected to our thoughts, and our thoughts are based on our beliefs.

Through this awareness, the destructive cycles we get caught in can be shifted. The most important place to start is recognising how we feel, naming our emotions and getting curious about how our feelings tie into our thoughts and beliefs.

Two important "keys" to help you explore your story:

- You are not your emotions
- You are not your thoughts!

In life, we can have negative connection with emotions:

- Emotions are bad.
- Emotions make you weak.
- Emotions are inappropriate.
- Emotions are not welcome in the workplace.
- Emotions make others uncomfortable.
- Emotions lead to shame.
- Emotions need to be shut away

Emotions are our body's way of telling us things. They are the moments when the beams of the lighthouse (learning about ourselves) illuminate something we need accept and explore to help us grow, connect and live a joyful, fulfilling life.

They are meant to be embraced, not disregarded.

The Feelings Wheel

References :
Gloria Willcox (1982) The Feeling Wheel, Transactional Analysis Journal,
12:4, 274-276, DOI: 10.1177/036215378201200411
Zinker, J. Creative process in gestalt therapy. Vintage Books, Random House, 1978.
Plutchick, R. Emotions: A psychorevolutionary synthesis. Harper and Row. 1980.
https://allthefeelz.app/cc/feeling-wheel/with UploadWizard

The feelings wheel is a visual we can use to understand how our emotions are making us feel and how that can ripple outward.

It is comprised of three circles with six primary feelings across those circles: Peaceful, Powerful, Joyful, Scared, Sad and Mad. The centre is where those six emotions start, and then the outer rings represent secondary and tertiary feelings that relate to those primary feelings.

Feelings are not good or bad; they simply are. They are the part of our body that tells us things about our thinking, our environment and our relationships.

Understanding the root emotion of your feelings can be crucial to understanding how to accept it and move forward.

Dr. Susan David, Psychologist at Harvard and author of best-selling book Emotional Agility, states:

"Incorrectly diagnosing our emotions and those of the people who surround us makes us respond incorrectly. We will take a different approach if we think we need to attend to anger than if we are handling disappointment or anxiety."

Additionally, if we don't acknowledge and connect with our emotions, we will reduce our physical health and increase our symptoms of stress.

If you access the allthefeelz.app, you will be able to work on your feelings to understand them better no matter where you are. If you want to get a better understanding of your thoughts and drivers, why not pop this wheel at your desk or in your wallet.

You can shift how you feel by changing your state (physically) by recognising your story or by choosing to be in that emotion because it's where you need to be right now.

Here is an example of how I used the feelings wheel to reflect on how I was feeling and use that information to embrace my emotions.

My Dad's Passing

I felt so sad, mad and scared. Those were my initial reactions. I felt depressed; I just wanted to hold my dad one last time and hear his voice, but it was covid, and he was in a coma. This sadness turned into grief and loss. Mad came up as I needed to accept that I would not be able to be at his funeral (Covid and a promise I made to him and my mother). Mad turned into hurt, and hurt into pain. I also felt scared because I was helpless to support my mother as she was grieving and trying to sort out the loose ends. Fear also led to more sadness and guilt.

The only way through the pain of these emotions was to recognise it, stay in it and then release it. I also needed to accept that things were out of my control. I choose to sit in my emotions and welcome them. I also went through the process of deep self-nurture and love.

I am still on this grieving journey. I am recognising that labelling my emotions, understanding them and releasing them allows me to learn from them and not get trapped. When I have done this, it has allowed me to understand myself, care for myself, and accept myself.

Practice 4

Recognising the Emotions You Feel

The next time you experience a heightened state of emotion, label that feeling and then sit back and reflect on the feelings and the thoughts driving that emotion. What could the beliefs be that are driving those thoughts? Learning how to sit with your emotions and not judge them as good or bad—just accept them as they are.

"NegativeEmotions...
They are the moments
when the beams of the
lighthouse (learning about
ourselves) illuminate
something we need accept
and explored to help us grow,
connect and live a joyful,
fulfilling life."

Stress in the Body

Nine years ago, I had just started my practice (Ignite Purpose). I was in complete survival mode even though I believed I had a purpose to make a difference; my purpose was tied up in my worth and my fear. I ignored my emotions, and I kept pushing myself harder. My fear stories were on a rampage, and their negative banter drove me forward, just like I had conditioned myself.

One day on a trip to the city to meet a potential client, I realised something was wrong. I had, as usual, rushed around at top speed and realised that I was starving. I popped into a sushi shop and purchased a Tuna and Avo sushi roll.

I was the mouse on the wheel, and I need the fuel to keep me moving. As I stood on the sidewalk of a busy Sydney street, I suddenly realised I couldn't breathe. I couldn't get the sushi down. It was stuck in my throat, and I thought I was choking. Yet, I wasn't choking I realised my throat was in a spasm, and I couldn't swallow. I had to calm down quickly or I would not be able to breathe. I slowly sat down on the sidewalk, took a few deep breaths and eventually swallowed. I realised I was not well, and I needed help.

I was diagnosed with Adrenal Fatigue and booked off work for three months. What I do know is that I still have bouts of fatigue, and they can be hard to manage, yet the more I am growing and taking care of myself, the less frequent they are.

I now listen to my body, which allows me to listen to my emotions; this, in turn, enables me to hear my thoughts and dig into my beliefs.

Recognising Signs of Stress

Stress can influence your entire body in a lot of different ways. Here are just a few of them:

- Brain - anxiety, irritability, depression, headaches and protection responses
- Heart - high blood pressure and cholesterol and increased risk of stroke or heart attack
- Stomach - acid reflux
- Oxygen levels - decreases cause shallow breathing and shortness of breath
- Muscles and Joints - aches, pain, tension and increased inflammation
- Skin - dry, flaky, irritated, pimples and rashes
- Hair - loss, brittle, dryness
- Immune System - decreased function, increased risk of sickness and longer recovery
- Gut - lower nutrient absorption, IBS, bloating, indigestion, pain and discomfort
- Reproductive system - decreased hormone production, decrease in libido and increase in PMS symptoms

Practice 5
Listen to Your Body:

Start to listen to your body. What physical sensations are you feeling, particularly during times of stress?

What stress triggers do you need to get curious about? How does it show up in your body? What can you do to reduce stress (what can you let go of) and increase peace of mind?

Reflection:

"My fear stories were on a rampage, and their negative banter drove me forward, just like I had conditioned myself."

*"If I love myself, I love you.
If I love you, I love myself."*

Loving Who You Are

In this story, I have shared how I needed to start my healing journey by getting to know myself and love myself. I needed to stop the hurt and pain that I would use to punish myself. I thought it was vain to love me, because it was against my belief of being humble.

After much growth I would rather believe that being humble is my ability to love myself deeply and thereby have great compassion and a deep connection with others to be better together.

If you can't love who you really are, how can you love and accept others? I love Rumi, and I want to share a few short poems and quotes with you that have supported me in my journey of loving myself:

- "Your task is not to seek for love, but merely to seek and find all the barriers within yourself that you have built against it."

- "Give yourself a kiss. If you want to hold the beautiful one, hold yourself."

- "The rose does best as a rose. Lilies make the best lilies. And look! You—the best you around!"

- "You are not a drop in the ocean. You are the entire ocean in a drop."

- "Don't be satisfied with stories, how things have gone with others. Unfold your own myth."

"Being humble is my ability to love myself deeply and thereby have great compassion and a deep connection with others to be better together"

Write Yourself a Love Letter

The final alchemy practice in this book is the opportunity to learn how to love yourself more deeply. I have learnt that in order to create intimacy with myself, I need to learn to love myself first. I run a program called Positive Intelligence (PQ) or Mental Fitness. This program was researched and designed by Shirzad Chamine. During the running of my first POD (group coaching session), I encountered a group of people who honoured me with their openness and growth.

With their permission, I am going to share the love letters they wrote to inspire you through their stories. To start, I will share the letter I wrote to myself:

Dear Tina,

What a beautiful smile you have. How could I forget how magical you are? Your rays of hope and love have often shone past the cold protection of the cage you have been trapped in...

Each bar of your cage was forged with fear, shame and the need to be loved. Tina, I have news for you...I love you. I love your chubby little legs, that beautiful brown skin, your fine curly hair that falls around your heart-shaped face. Those big brown eyes sparkle with Joy and Delight!

Thank you for whispering HOPE in my ears when all I could see were the bars that locked you in. Thank you for shining through when I felt I couldn't take one more breath...you whispered I need to look up...my purpose and calling aren't finished yet. Your little hands outstretched between the fear and shame bars calling out to Mommy and Daddy to help, to free you/me...

Yet Tina, the journey of life was already set in motion. With love, I now reach up and free Tina, that has only shown herself in sm all moments. Tina, your mom and dad have always loved you. Tina, I love you, I slowly bend down and pick up your small brown hand. I whisper back to you...

Shine, Tina, shine...I can't complete the journey, the mission, the calling without you shining...

It's your time Tina, awake and be free.

7 Letters of Love

Dear Me 1

I am writing to remind you what an amazing person you are!

You grew up in an environment where not much love or care was given, and you assumed that was because you were not good enough and had to prove yourself just to be accepted and loved.

You continued your whole life with this mindset...in order to be liked, loved, accepted, you had to achieve...otherwise what was the point of your existence??

Please let me remind you that you ARE worthy of love! You are a kind, smart, loving and compassionate person, with a positive outlook on life.

I admire the way you continue to challenge yourself, learning new things along the way and learning from mistakes.

You should never care what people think of you. You absolutely do deserve a seat at the table.

You are a good mum, wife, leader, always seeing the best in others and encouraging others in their journeys.

You are worthy, you are valuable, you are loved, you are enough...just allow yourself to be you, Me

Dear Me 2

Do you remember when you were very young and in the old house? Do you remember being in that warm cocoon of family love?

You were so happy and carefree then. It might be just the old photo that reminds me, but I think I can recall you at 8 months old, enjoying being washed in a tub of warm water in the sunroom with the early morning light flooding through. You still love the cascade of warm water when you shower.

I do distinctly remember the warm spring day when you were playing in the garden on your own, perhaps about 2, smelling the flowers and oozing happiness. You still love spring and the warmth of the sun after winter.

So, when did things start to change? When did you start to care what others thought about you or how they might judge you and how you could be hurt?

I do remember the sleepless night when you were 6 after your teacher announced that she would check the reading cards the next day, and you feared that you would be found out as you had not completed them correctly. I remember how frightened you were that you would get into trouble and how your parents were so worried that you wouldn't tell them what was wrong. I also remember how you concocted a plan to disguise it and it worked, and so started a pattern of creating the perfect façade to hide the real you.

For many years you kept up the pretense to the outside

world. Many people found you as cold and uncaring, as you rarely shared the real you. Little did they know what was going on inside.

The cancer diagnosis changed so many things and for the better. You came back to you. You appreciated real life and what is important. You started to really observe and love nature again, the animals, the trees, the sky and of course the spring flowers. You let other people in, and you started to reach out to them.

You're still on your journey, but know that I love you for all your flaws and imperfections. You are perfectly imperfect, and let all the world know it.

Dear Me 3

Hi to that happy, energetic, cheeky, curious me...We go back a long way, to the very beginning of life. We are connected in a way no one will or could ever understand. We have been there, standing together. Sometimes crying in the shower but it has always been you and me.

However, some time ago I left you. I left you floundering on your own to rely on love and encouragement and strength from others when it was I who should have held you up. When it was me who should have hugged you praised and appreciated you for the individual you are—for all the life you bring to the world.

I rarely tell you how much I admire you. How caring and intelligent and strong you are. You are my hero!

I should have told you not to care what others think. To not be afraid to be different. To not be ashamed of who you are. Worst of all I should have cared what people thought because in doing so, I said horrible things to shame you. I took you for granted and dishonoured you. I said you were not enough.

You do not need anyone else's approval or friendship to be whole. Together we are enough. We will conquer this new future.

I've got you and this time I am not letting you go. This time I will put you first.

I will respect you, honour and cherish who you are!
ME

Dear Me 4

As you wake up today, you have the ocean as your view. For a few days now you have been watching the waves come to shore and hit and break against the rocks, and you realise this was your life for a long time. Rolling with tides in your life—high tides when your life was uncontrolled, then low tides when it was calm. The high tides were forming you. You ARE the rocks. Strong, unmovable, but the water shaped you just as it smooth the rock's edges, It smoothed and shaped you.

Today I want to tell you don't be afraid of the high tide or the rough sea anymore, because it always calms down again. You have taught yourself to ride the waves of change. You have added enough salty tears to add to the ocean. I love that a great movie or gift or words can stir your heart to happy tears. It means you care; it signifies the softness in you. You value people and friendships—true friendships.

From your first breath, things were difficult. You had to fight to take your first breath. You were meant to be here. Maybe to show others that no matter how many deep breaths you need to take, just breathe! No matter what!

You've set high standards for yourself, which didn't serve you well at times, because you have to just BE! Don't be what others expect you to be—JUST BE!

Just be your authentic self—that's good enough.

You've already arrived—you don't have to prove anything anymore. You have what so many people wish for today. You have a loving and successful marriage. Yes girl, you held on and fought for that dream and here you are, married for 26 years already. You have raised beautiful boys—you can be so proud of them, yes breathe you did that!

You are creative and innovative, and people love what your creativity brings. It's made so many people smile before.

You love making people feel special and you give the greatest gifts and presents because you listen, you observe and that makes people feel valued. Don't worry about your fluffy body, or dimples, you deserve it. And it doesn't define you. You are a great sister, friend, mom, daughter, mentor, wife and the list goes on. You see, you are Royalty—you also have a title, and you wear those crowns proudly. So today, my dear little brave girl, enjoy your life, play in the waves, build sandcastles, run with your babies, laugh infectiously be happy, be brave, be loving, BE YOU.

Love,

Me

Dear Me 5

I think you are doing a sensational job of enjoying your life.

You are positive, strong-willed, determined, honest, loving, empathetic and smart. We have such fun together. Every day we have on this planet is a gift, and we have grown the most wonderful family, and it's such fun being in our life.

You are interested in other people and intrigued by their stories; you don't judge them, you see them and hear them and value them and their contributions to life and society. You learn from mistakes with grace and enjoy feedback as it is a learning experience—even when it is critical, you're able to see the gift in it, and use that to better yourself.

You save money and live a frugal life, but spend that money on things that will give you memories to treasure and experiences to enhance this great journey. You don't want things and stuff to make you happy; you want connection and love. You do lots of continuing personal growth activities to make your life and the life of your family and friends a rich, interesting place to be.

You have such an abundance of ideas, and you are not worried about the thoughts of other people...I really like that you don't feel concerned about their judgement, as it is not of consequence to you. You keep having ideas and doing what you can to use them to make life an easier more productive place to be.

You love your job and work, not for what you do, but how what you do makes you feel, and the amazing relationships you have at work. You spend time with people that lift you up, doing adventurous things, breaking new ground, tasting new things and confidently moving away from those that don't fill your bucket—for this, I am proud of you.

Life with you is calm and relaxing, but full and enjoyable. We meditate, we enjoy the sunshine, we dance in the rain and cuddle cold gum trees on our bush walks. You support the people around you with a never-ending message from your heart...and you know that sometimes you are full-on with your enthusiasm and ideas, and it can be annoying...but those that love it know how to manage you and keep you around as you show them your love fiercely!

I hope that I can look back at my letter to me in the years to come and still value myself and my direction as much as I do today. I know that parts of my journey have been challenging, but I don't honestly remember them...so we do well to not judge our past and only to look forward together to everything that we get to do in life.

I hope that our kids grow to be the balanced, judgement-free, curious, loving, empathetic, kind, thoughtful, fun-loving, enjoyable people that you are, too.

Love ya! x

Dear Me 6

I look at the old photograph, just slightly faded with time. I see the little boy, the little me, his golden curly hair with an infectious smile and twinkling blue eyes. I see you, old friend. I look down at my hands worn by the passing of time, and I remember the tiny hands of the boy I once was. What a way we have come, old friend. What stories we can tell, adventures lived, heartbreak endured, but here we are.

I look into your little eyes, and although you are smiling for the world, I know that look. I carry it still. If you know where to focus in the eyes, the sadness, just on the edge of perception. You had so many dreams, dreams in which you would be good enough, clever enough, accepted and loved. Your confidence veiled all your insecurities, hid your loneliness and sadness from the world. You hid your anxieties behind humour, acting the clown and making others laugh. At the same time, inside, there was nothing but a cavern filled with tears.

We fought the world together, little man, even though the odds were stacked against us. We found love, lost love, endured failure and defeat. We have mourned, and we have had fleeting moments of happiness.

Thank you for walking this road with me, little friend. You have always been there; you have been my constant companion in the heat, cold, light and darkness. When I faced overwhelming challenges and was at the point of giving up, you were the little courageous voice, deep inside driving me on with your relentless defiance of the world.

As I look at your little beaming face in the picture once again, I have a secret to tell you. The old man in me can do it now. You are good enough, little man, you always were. You didn't have to achieve it. You just were imperfectly perfect, so rest easy deep inside my soul and rest.

Dear Me 7

You know I have been with you even before you were born!

I saw your brave battle when you almost did not make it through birth. Right there and then, I knew that your life must have a special meaning!

And rightfully so...your parent's named you Amanda, which means "worthy of love".

When you were small, you stole hearts, not only with your green eyes and blond hair...you were gentle and kind, cared about others. You adapted to various circumstances quickly and were easygoing. You were always "up for fun", even if it entailed some degree of naughtiness.

At 5, your mother walked to school with you to enrol you, and you kept telling her to go home. At 5 you went away with neighbours you did not know for so long that you demonstrated strong independence.

As you grew older, life threw various degrees of unexpected "curveballs" at you. But you lifted your head and continued the journey. Some people said you had a "rebellious spirit" and wanted to do "deliverance" on you. But you lifted your head once again and moved forward, knowing deep inside, there must be another answer.

At times you were different; sometimes you tried to fit in, and other times just went along being true to yourself.

It all came together when you did the 8 dimensions thinking preferences profiles and was introduced to Brain

Gym from Dr. Paul Dennison. It was like WOW! I have finally arrived! For the first time, your true self was understood...!!!

Through the years of being curious and inquisitive, you have studied, done courses, looked at DVDs, listened to CDs. But very important, you were willing to learn from your mistakes and had a teachable spirit.

Now you have a basket full of amazing things to help you on your journey ahead.

The world is yet to see the fullness of who you are as a person and how you will bring everything together for good...

Me xx

Practice 6
Loving Who You Are

Imagine receiving a letter from yourself to yourself that retells the story of who you are.

You can stay stuck in a dark place, where your shame, disappointments and hurt live. Where you can't believe you said something, did something, created or even lived a horrible situation.

We, as humans, are wired to protect ourselves. At times we make decisions that seem the best ones for our survival. Sometimes these are not "nice", "good", or "beautiful" stories, so we hide and struggle to make peace with them.

We keep punishing ourselves, which stops us from owning it for what it is and forgiving ourselves, acknowledging we did the best we could at that moment.

Or you can reconnect with your inner child and remind yourself of all the goodness you bring to the world.

This love letter is for you and you alone; it's for you to recognise who you really are and to choose to see your life as a gift. Acceptance and love will allow you to be all you are.

Use an old photo of you when you were young, free and open to all things if it would help you visualize the YOU that still lives. Consider the best of you and write your own love letter to yourself. You are worth acceptance, love, compassion, kindness, joy and hope. You are the author of your story.

Practice: *Dear Me.....*

Final Thoughts

We are all on a journey in our lives. I look back at my journey, and I find many lessons and insights. However, I am most grateful that I have learned how to be present and hold my own space with courage.

I have learnt that fear loses its hold on me only when I see my shame and recognise it. I have also learnt that I needed to share my story to be free. I have started owning my worthiness as a unexchangeable part of me. I am good enough for love and belonging.

I am wrapping my arms around learning about myself and my life every day. I am determined to be the best of who I already am, which means I need to shed some of the fear and armour I have carried with me for years. I am on a continual, beautiful journey.

I hope that the story of the Glass Angel, my story and the alchemy practices bring you to your next level of growth and help you live a more purposeful, peaceful and engaged life.

Please join me on social media and stay connected to my world. I create regular live streams and have podcasts. I also coach, lead and teach people how to be better together.

Finally, I love Dr Maya Angelou and will leave you with her words on love—after all, we need to make sure we own the source that feeds our thinking and behaviour.

"Love recognises no barriers. It jumps hurdles, leaps fences, penetrates walls to arrive at its destination full of hope."

I send you love.

Christina